Leadership
and the Quest
for Integrity

LEADERSHIP
AND THE QUEST
FOR INTEGRITY

Joseph L. Badaracco, Jr.
Richard R. Ellsworth

Harvard Business School Press
Boston, Massachusetts

Originally published in hardcover by the
Harvard Business School Press, 1989

Printed in the United States of America

02   5

Library of Congress Cataloging-in-Publication Data

Badaracco, Joseph.
  Leadership and the quest for integrity.

  Bibliography: p. 211
  Includes index.
  1. Leadership.   I. Ellsworth, Richard R.   II. Title.
HD57.7.B33   1988   658.4'092   88-24507
ISBN 0-87584-408-1

The paper used in this publication meets the requirements of the
American National Standard for Permanence of Paper for printed
Library Materials Z39.49-1984.

This book is dedicated to our parents

Joseph and Valeria Badaracco
Melvin and Aladine Ellsworth

CONTENTS

ACKNOWLEDGMENTS

We owe great debts to the many people who helped us develop our understanding of leadership. Our work together began at the Harvard Business School. We set out to create a version of Business Policy, a required "capstone" course addressing the work and responsibilities of general managers, that would explicitly address the question: What leads to outstanding performance as a manager? We found we could not answer the question fully without making a major effort to understand leadership. We received considerable initial encouragement and continued support in this effort from J. Ronald Fox, John Matthews, and Malcolm Salter, three of our colleagues at Harvard. Ronald Fox took a particular interest in our work, urging us on and constructively challenging our thinking. The ideas and comments of Abraham Zaleznik were also instrumental in the critical early phases of the work.

Once we decided to expand these efforts into a book, we were fortunate to have the cooperation of seven chief executives who committed their time to help us better understand the foundations of leadership. They are: Alexander d'Arbeloff, Ralph E. Bailey, James E. Burke, Reuben Mark, J. Richard Munro, Irving S. Shapiro, and Walter Wriston. We have great respect for these men and are grateful for their interest, openness, and candor and for sharing with us the rich understanding of leadership they had derived from many years of experience and reflection.

We are indebted to others who read all or parts of the manuscript at various stages of its four-year development. Their comments helped us refine our thinking in many critical areas. In addition to those mentioned above, we appreciate the contributions made by Kenneth Andrews, James Heskett, Paul Lawrence, Thomas McCraw, Don Miller, Andrall Pearson,

James Brian Quinn, Leonard Sayles, Howard Stevenson, and Renato Tagiuri. We have also drawn heavily upon the intellectual heritage created by Peter Drucker at The Claremont Graduate School and by those who developed the field of business policy at the Harvard Business School—Frank Aguilar, Kenneth Andrews, Christopher Bartlett, Norman Berg, Joseph Bower, C. Roland Christensen, Richard Hamermesh, John Matthews, Malcolm Salter, Bruce Scott, Howard Stevenson, and Michael Yoshino.

This manuscript also benefited in immeasurable ways from what we have learned from three other sources. The managers we worked with before we entered academia provided the opportunity for the best research possible—firsthand personal experience with executives of exceptional skill. We also learned a great deal from the chief executives who helped us write cases about their companies and shared their perspectives on management with us, particularly Adam Aronson, Leo Benatar, E. H. Clark, Jr., Edward Hennessy, Peter Viele, and Hans Wyss. Finally, our students at Claremont and Harvard helped us clarify our thoughts through their challenging questions and insights.

We are especially grateful to those who devoted so many hours to the task of making this manuscript a reality: to Sarah Markham, whose friendship, commitment, and administrative and secretarial skills par excellence helped in nearly every facet of the project; to Cheryl Handel, whose editorial support was careful, probing, and incisive; and to Eliza Collins, our editor at the Harvard Business School Press, whose creativity, skill, and keen understanding of our message made an invaluable contribution to this book.

Above all, we are indebted to our families. Our mothers and fathers taught us much about leading lives of integrity. Both our fathers are accomplished leaders. Joseph Badaracco, an attorney by profession, has been a leader in the civic and political life of St. Louis, Missouri, inspiring many others through his thoughtful, determined, candid, and often courageous efforts to contribute to the lives of its citizens. Melvin Ellsworth's faith in the ability of others, his fairness, and his sense of purpose have left an indelible impact on those who have known him. His uncompromising commitment to excellence enabled him to rise to become president of the Fluor Corporation, leading it to a place of distinction in the book *In Search of Excellence*. Without the abiding support, encouragement, and understanding of our wives, Mary Anne and Ginger, this book would not have become a reality.

Finally, we are grateful to each other for the commitment, openness, patience, and especially the friendship that has grown out of our work together.

Joseph L. Badaracco, Jr.   Richard R. Ellsworth
Boston, Massachusetts   Claremont, California

June 1988

Leadership
and the Quest
for Integrity

PART I

LEADERSHIP PHILOSOPHIES

INTRODUCTION

Why is it so hard for managers to create the kind of teams, departments, and companies that they want? Managers know what an ideal organization is. Its goals are clear, it innovates, attracts high-caliber talent, challenges them with high standards, and promotes on the basis of merit. The ideal organization is immune to bureaucracy. It is ethical and inspiring. Its economic performance is outstanding.

Few managers live and work in this ideal, ethereal realm. For most of them, daily work is a messy reality of trade-offs and dilemmas. The reason is simple. The problems and questions that reach senior managers usually cannot be answered by specialized techniques or skills. Otherwise, they would have been delegated to someone else. In real organizations, the most difficult, anxiety-provoking, and dilemma-ridden problems rise to the top.

In this world of gray areas and judgment calls, managers need guidance—some way of resolving dilemmas—in order to build the kind of organizations they want. This book provides such guidance, for it is a book about leadership. It answers the question of what distinguishes the men and women who create extraordinary organizations from workaday professional managers. Managers who build records of achievement do so through the ways in which they resolve dilemmas. These are the difficult issues of thought and action that test all managers and separate leaders from capable, dependable managers. They also distinguish bright, idea-driven people who merely dream from hands-on leaders who figure out how, when, and whether something should be done, and then do it.

We argue that managers are much more likely to excel if they approach their dilemmas with certain prejudices. We use "prejudice" in its literal sense. That is, we believe managers should approach dilemmas with preconceived biases toward handling them in certain ways. The rationale for these prejudices is a quest for integrity, an effort that is at once moral, philosophical, and practical—for it strives to achieve coherence among a manager's daily actions, personal values, and basic aims for his or her organization.

This book differs greatly from much of the conventional wisdom on leadership and management. Many people believe that leadership is essentially a matter of charisma—a rare, elusive, transforming characteristic that sets leaders apart and impels others to follow them. This view is not false, but it is sorely inadequate and misleading. If leadership rests on a barely describable trait of a handful of men and women, then others must resign themselves to simply plodding forward in their appointed tasks. Worse, reducing leadership to charisma ignores the facts. The vast majority of business leaders have succeeded, not through charisma, but through experience, judgment, boldness, tenacity, and hard work. By itself, charisma is neither necessary nor sufficient for business leadership.

Another common view is that training in professional management can help managers achieve outstanding results. This idea waxes and wanes. During the 1960s and 1970s, when the ideas and techniques of professional management took hold in U.S. industry, it was widely accepted. Management was no longer considered a practical art, learned through patient experience and enhanced by the elusive qualities of judgment and insight. Instead, management was deemed almost a science, complete with its own techniques: strategic planning systems, portfolio analysis, elaborate capital budgeting mechanisms, sophisticated organizational design, tailored measurement and reward systems, and computerized information systems.

While it is now fashionable to criticize professional management, it has made vital contributions to the management of companies. As markets, competitors, and companies have grown increasingly complicated, reliance on intuition and back-of-the-envelope analysis proved inadequate. The new concepts and analytical frameworks have given managers greater ability to sort out the sometimes bewildering complexities facing them. New techniques have encouraged more rational choices about strategic objectives, helped push common goals down into the organization, allocated resources in a more focused way, channeled information and delegated authority to those who could use it best, and provided top management with greater control over decision making.

Yet the performance resulting from professional management has often proved disappointing. Instead of leading to outstanding company performance, its adoption has paralleled our competitive decline. Why? In part, this is because a small, intensely competitive, aggressive industry has emerged in which consultants, planners, academics, and publishers rapidly disseminate the latest versions of modern scientific management. Each year, more than sixty thousand MBAs graduate, thousands of managers complete executive education programs, business books detailing the latest techniques climb near the top of bestseller lists, companies spend billions of dollars on consulting fees, and thousands of executives migrate among companies. As a result, management techniques are rapidly transferred within an increasingly fluid market— and the advantage gained from applying the latest techniques is, at best, transient.

In their preoccupation with technique, many professional managers and business academics have made management so complicated that they miss some obvious yet critical aspects of business leadership. The extraordinary success of In Search of Excellence—one of the bestselling books of all times— is powerful evidence of a certain hollowness in the notion of professional management. Many academics, consultants, and opinion leaders in the professional management industry scoffed at the book. Yet the critics ignored the real reasons for its success: its many inspiring stories of committed individuals and their followers. These were tales of impassioned business leaders, not cool professional technocrats. The book's enormous sales were a populist revolt against management theoreticians, academics, and professionals. Management technique is useful, sometimes critical, but it is no surrogate for leadership. Vision is not reflected in portfolio planning charts. Few people leave for work in the morning invigorated by the thought of maximizing net present values.

Along with charisma and professional management, we reject a third commonplace view of outstanding management. It may be summarized in three words: "It all depends." That is, the situations that managers face vary so dramatically that the right action for a manager depends almost exclusively on the particulars of a situation—on the company strategy, the politics and personalities of the situation, the organization, and so forth. As a result, a manager's "style" should vary from situation to situation. The best managers are those who have the widest repertories of styles and are the most adept at matching styles to situations.

The style school is riddled with problems. One is that most managers simply aren't very good at switching styles. All of us are creatures of habit, experience, and personality. Moreover, if a manager has peers, bosses, and subordinates who are intelligent and perceptive, and if a manager works with them closely on vexing problems, they all will come to know the manager well. In such circumstances, it is impossible to mask one's real beliefs, values, and thinking.

The biggest deficiency of the style school, however, is that it provides no guidance whatsoever for resolving the dilemmas managers face. It leaves them completely on their own, facing an unending stream of complex, sometimes bewildering problems without a map to guide their decisions and actions.

In the end, there is a single powerful reason why charisma, professional management, and style are inadequate ways for managers to approach and resolve the dilemmas they face. Resolving dilemmas involves a person's philosophy of management. Whether they believe it or not, all managers have them. These philosophies are tacit, not explicit. The philosophies involve fundamental assumptions about human nature, about people in organizations, about the work of managers, and the kind of activities that lead to outstanding results. Like a geological deposit, these tacit philosophies build up over many years through the experiences and influences that shape a person's life. Few managers stop, reflect on, and make explicit their philosophies of management and leadership. But these deep assumptions influence almost everything they do.

The first part of this book describes three of the most common philosophies of management. Each is an internally consistent set of assumptions about human nature, people in organizations, the work of managers, and the ways leaders should work day-by-day. Each philosophy reflects traditions of thought that reach back several centuries as well as contemporary ideas raised frequently in the business press and in MBA classrooms. Yet the philosophies clash with each other and offer conflicting advice to managers.

Each of the three chapters in Part I explains and strongly advocates one of the three philosophies. We call these three philosophies *political* leadership, *directive* leadership, and *values-driven* leadership. We deliberately wrote each of these chapters to advocate one of the philosophies. Our aim is to engage you viscerally as well as intellectually. We wanted to challenge directly your personal beliefs and help you understand your own implicit ideas about business leadership. Ideally, you will confront the assumptions and behavior that each philosophy advocates and contrast them with your own beliefs and ways of working. Ask yourself: Do I agree with these assumptions? Is this how I manage or want to manage? Does this philosophy describe the executives I really admire? Which philosophy offers the surest path to leadership?

As you read and react to these philosophies, you will find that they conflict with each other and raise two critical, practical questions: Does one or another of the philosophies offer better guidance to managers? How can the philosophies help managers to resolve the dilemmas they face?

In Part II, we answer these questions by analyzing five of the most important dilemmas that managers face. The first is the tension between general, flexible, open-ended approaches to problems and precise, clear approaches. The

second is the tension between top-down and bottom-up influence on important decisions. To what extent, for instance,
should managers intervene in their subordinates' activities?
What role should they allow others to play in making
decisions?

The third dilemma is the conflict between substance
and process. Concentrating on substance means working
directly to get the right answer to a problem. Concentrating
on process means working on the right *way* of getting the
answer.

The fourth dilemma, between confrontation and compromise, arises whenever conflicts occur in an organization—
in other words, daily. Almost anything can be the focus of a
conflict: minor issues such as who gets what office as well as
major ones such as setting strategic goals.

Because it takes so many different forms, the last dilemma is difficult to describe in a single, short phrase. Put
most succinctly, it is the tension between tangibles and intangibles. The familiar form of the dilemma is the choice between
short-term and long-term considerations. Tangible considerations, such as good relations with people a manager works with,
urgent requests from customers, and budgets and quotas can,
and often do, collide with subtler, more distant considerations, such as personal ethical values, a company's social obligations, and its broad strategic aims.

In Part II, we show that managers are much more
likely to achieve exceptional results if they approach their
dilemmas with certain fundamental prejudices. Managers
should have biases toward resolving dilemmas in certain
ways.

The notion of "prejudices" acknowledges the intrinsic, inescapable messiness of many of the problems managers face. Rules, techniques, or cookie-cutter approaches devised to fit all situations won't work. But certain ways of
thinking and acting are more likely to lead to outstanding
performance. The prejudices that we advocate in the last part
of the book are practical guides to resolving the dilemmas we
have described. The demands of situations do vary, so the

prejudices are strong preferences, not hard-and-fast rules. At times, managers will need to override the prejudices we describe, but they should do so only cautiously, infrequently, and reluctantly.

The notion of prejudices avoids two traps into which much of the writing about business management and leadership has fallen. The first trap is trying to give specific, precise rules for outstanding management. Because this approach ignores the diversity and messiness of managers' problems, it is doomed. The second trap is oversimplification. Some writers pitch their advice in such broad and general terms that their recommendations are vacant or mere platitudes. The style school epitomizes this approach.

The prejudices provide guidance to managers who have a vision or a plan and want to know how to make it a reality or modify and improve it by drawing on the judgment and creativity of the people they work with.

Why are the prejudices we advocate the right approach? What makes them the best guide for resolving dilemmas and for thinking through the conflicting philosophies of leadership that pull managers in different directions? The answer to this question lies in understanding what integrity means for managers.

The word "integrity" is familiar but its meaning is complex. In fact, all of Part II is an explanation of the role that integrity plays in leadership. In essence, integrity is consistency between what a manager believes, how a manager acts, and a manager's aspiration for his or her organization. But not any consistency will do. An incompetent or corrupt manager can be perfectly consistent. But certain beliefs, actions, and aspirations are much more likely than others to lead to outstanding results. The prejudices we advocate reflect these beliefs. Actions based on the prejudices simply translate these beliefs into practice—in the uncertain, often turbulent life of managers. In short, prejudices are a way of making integrity alive, powerful, and effective in a world of dilemmas and conflicting philosophies of management.

This argument is based upon a wide range of evidence and ideas. It rests, first of all, on our own experience working in companies, consulting for them, and writing in-depth case studies about their strategies and management. We have taught literally hundreds of cases about companies of all sizes as members of the faculty of The Claremont Graduate School and the Harvard Business School and have discussed the issues they raised with many of our colleagues, in some instances over many years. We have also drawn upon the many books and articles that discuss business leadership. In fact, the three philosophies of leadership are, among other things, our way of sorting out the basic themes that run through this body of literature.

We tested and refined our conclusions through exten-sive discussions with seven senior executives, each widely respected for records of achievement. These were Alexander d'Arbeloff, co-founder and president of Teradyne; Ralph E. Bailey, former chairman of Conoco; James E. Burke, chairman of Johnson & Johnson; Reuben Mark, president of Colgate-Palmolive; J. Richard Munro, CEO of Time Inc.; Irving S. Sha-piro, the former chairman of Du Pont; and Walter Wriston, former chairman of Citicorp.

Some of these men are retired, while others are likely to head their companies for the rest of the century. Their in-dustries range from those of mature industrial America to high-technology, include both products and services, and face competition both overseas and at home. The interviews were confidential, generally lasted three hours or longer, and ranged across many topics. Throughout our conversations, we listened carefully for ideas, convictions, attitudes, experi-ences, and decisions that cast light on the basic questions of leadership. At an introspective moment in one interview, we were told, "This is like going to your psychiatrist." Our aim was not to generate systematic data or conclusive answers to questions that have long bedeviled scholars, essayists, man-agers, and teachers. Instead, we sought to gain a deeper under-standing of the issues the three philosophies of leadership raise.

These leaders were not chosen as exemplars of the

three philosophies. Rather, we wanted to use them as sounding boards and understand their thinking about basic philosophies of leadership. All of them had reflected on the issues we raised and that is why they all contributed so greatly to the ideas in this book. Above all, they helped convince us that thinking about leadership in terms of dilemmas, prejudices, and integrity is a powerful source of guidance for managers who want to make a difference.

Chapter 1

POLITICAL LEADERSHIP

How do you change things? You can issue directives.
Some people will respond, but some people will go do
something else. Or you can try to win the organization
over and convince people that what you're doing makes
sense for the future. I chose the latter course. Without
the support of the organization, I would have been dead.

> Irving S. Shapiro,
> former chairman, Du Pont

You are selling all the time. I don't care whether you call
it politics or not, it's appealing to someone's basic self-
interest. It's Dale Carnegie, chapter one, paragraph one
without question. You are selling all the time.

> Confidential statement from
> the chairman of a successful
> *Fortune* 500 company

Everybody is always looking one or two levels up and
asking, "How do I get there?" You can't do anything
about this. The level of tea leaf reading is constant.

> J. Richard Munro, CEO,
> Time Inc.

Thousands of capable professional managers work
hard, only to produce industry-average returns for their companies. Yet a handful of outstanding managers lead their companies to superior performance. What distinguishes these two
groups?

The quotations above—from widely respected heads

13

of major companies—point toward one answer to that question. Put bluntly, *outstanding managers are astute organizational politicians.* They have powerful, creative ideas about their companies and industries. But to reduce destructive internal resistance to their ideas, they do not pursue their visions head on. They keep their goals broad, flexible, and sometimes even vague, and they move incrementally, patiently, and often obliquely to translate their goals into reality.

In doing so, they part company with the conventional image of business leaders as commanding father figures or heroes in action. They are hard-headed realists about organizational life. This is why we call this philosophy of leadership "political leadership." "Political" best describes both the reality of organizations as well as a central task of management: gaining power over the forces of self-interest that sow seeds of conflict and division within a company.

The ultimate aim of these leaders' incremental moves and political sensitivities is to translate vision into reality. Day-by-day, this approach demands subtlety, patience, and sophistication. It requires skill at the art of implementation. But it does not presuppose amoral, Machiavellian opportunism. Machiavelli's ideal prince was willing to play the fox, to disguise his own character, and to deceive others in order to accomplish his ends. There is no question that politically astute managers can be selfish and manipulative. However, the political philosophy of leadership that we describe is practiced by many well-intentioned, honest leaders in pursuit of their companies' best interests, not personal gain. They realize leadership involves acquiring the power to channel the political forces in an organization toward common objectives.

Why is a politically oriented philosophy desirable? After all, some thinkers view companies as harmonious communities of benevolent individuals who join ranks to pursue strategic goals determined by rational analysis. Organizational realists disagree. Outstanding managers must be astute organizational politicians because a company is often a political arena—not some sort of ideal family. People in companies jockey, push, and bargain to advance their interests and those of the units they head. In our interviews with senior executives this basic trait of company life surfaced time and time again.

This chapter sets forth the assumptions underlying political leadership and describes its practical implications. It shows how outstanding leaders, sensitive to organizational politics and acting incrementally, accomplish the basic tasks of management: setting and communicating goals, managing systems and organizational structures, resolving conflicts, and handling the daily work of running a business.

THE PHILOSOPHY OF POLITICAL LEADERSHIP

Political leadership as a philosophy of management rests on certain fundamental assumptions about human nature and about the way people behave in companies. These assumptions fall in two categories: the splintering forces that diffuse a company's efforts and the inertial forces that make companies bureaucratic and resistant to change.

The Splintering Forces

The first powerful splintering force that diffuses efforts within an organization is self-interest, the dominant motivator of human behavior. The second is scarcity of resources, which creates zero-sum battles—"I win, you lose"— for capital and people. Third, intensifying competition outside and complexity inside companies call for increased specialization. This fragments authority and disperses skills and information. It also leads people to see the world from their unit's perspective and do what is best for their unit. Fourth, when subunits genuinely try to act in the broad interest of their company, they often do so on the basis of their own local perceptions, which can easily be out of line with a company's overall needs.

Self-Interest and the Pursuit of Power. Powerful splintering forces originate in the natural human tendency to seek personal advancement. In companies, this drive leads people to make decisions, interpret information, and take actions that serve their personal interests and those of the sub-units (product units, functional areas, geographic units, and staff areas) in which they work. They do this by gaining and exercising power.

Simply defined, power is the ability to influence others and to avoid being influenced by them. It flows from several sources.[1] A formal position in an organization can confer authority to establish goals, control key functional policies, allocate money, assign personnel, hire and fire, and set salaries. Expertise grants people the power to control important information and judgments regarding critical decisions. Even simple affection or respect for someone can increase his or her power. People try hard to accumulate power because power is "money in the bank," a currency to be spent to further advance individual interest. When members of an organization harness these sources of power to their personal ends, local self-interest rather than strategic objectives can drive much of a company's activity.

Competition for Scarce Resources. Corporate financial policies, such as capital structure and dividend policies, limit how much capital a company can spend. Usually, heads of divisions or functional areas have little influence over these policies. Hence, they often become political. Negotiating for a larger piece of the available capital pie becomes more important than pressing senior management to raise more money—a battle they have little prospect of winning.

Reflecting on how little divisional managers resisted a proposal to cut his company's capital spending, a senior executive observed:

> The general managers who had substantial capital needs believed that they would be successful in privately lobbying corporate management for additional funds. Each

manager tended to believe that it would be the other divisions, not his own, that would be curtailed.[2]

Divisive, time-consuming, behind-the-scenes maneuvering is often the device used to further local interests.

Specialization and the Fragmentation of Authority. Political leaders do not view this self-interested behavior as an aberration or a pathology. They see it as a fact of organizational life. Other facts are fragmentation of authority and increasing complexity. These nurture the seeds that self-interest has sown.

To allow important decisions to be made by those with the relevant expertise and information, influence over important decisions is dispersed among many people. This process not only helps a company respond faster to changing conditions, but also increases managers' and employees' satisfaction and commitment. But the range of differing expertise, the variety of needed skills, and the necessity for multiple layers of managers all fragment power and authority.

This fragmentation increases with a company's size, the range of its products and businesses, and the geographic scope of its operations. In recent years, business has grown far more complicated. Unpredictable technological changes, increased and varied overseas activities, and webs of rules and regulations imposed by governments all challenge managers' ability to stay on top of their operations. At the same time, management techniques have grown more complicated. Portfolio planning, discounted cash-flow analysis, and other analytical techniques have become part of the standard operations and decision making in many companies.

Each area of complexity requires specialists to study it, manage it, and report on it to others. The proliferation of specialized expertise further complicates companies. Moreover, each area of expertise becomes another potential source of subunit self-interest. Functional specialists develop their own goals and loyalties: "be the best sales force no matter what," or "keep marketing from fouling up production."

These specialists can perceive the same external or internal challenges quite differently because they have different skills, responsibilities, and career stakes. Their differences in perspective and judgment are heightened by genuine misunderstandings caused by the imperfect flow of information. This occurs in even the best-managed companies.

Conflicts inevitably arise between specialized units. Talented and ambitious people often clash with each other as they attempt to do their jobs and to protect and expand their jurisdictions. Conflicts between line and staff are legendary. Paradoxically, the better a company's managers are, the greater the dispersion of power and the risk of conflicts can be. Pushing for autonomy and the responsibility that comes with it, they expect senior managers to respect their track records and to let them run their operations as they judge best. Of course, a tough senior executive can run roughshod over their preferences. But he or she does so only at substantial risk.

Reflecting on several decades of his own experience, Irving Shapiro said:

> I am not convinced that you move strong people by direct commands. My experience has been quite the other way—that planting seeds and fertilizing them, and letting the other fellow harvest the crop, very often makes greater progress than a direct command. This is because of the way strong people are put together. They have a great pride in their own intellect and accomplishments. They want to be the inventor and the man of action and not have things imposed on them. Intellectually, they will accept it if you tell them to do something, but emotionally they'll resent it. So we're really dealing with the question of how you best move a strong man, a strong subordinate.

As a company becomes more complex, the information senior executives get is filtered by the managers and specialists below them. It becomes condensed, quantitative, and abstract. Because they have greater expertise and are closer to products and markets, they take the initiative in identifying problems and opportunities, devising alternatives, and choosing among them. A leader hence becomes less an originator of new ideas. In the words of one executive: "If you have some knowledge of the nitty-gritty of a business, you can affect others' business decisions. But an awful lot is an act of faith."

Localitis. Conflict often arises from genuine but differing convictions about the nature of problems and the way to resolve them. General George C. Marshall called this "localitis." That is, "the conviction ardently held by every theater commander that the war was being won or lost in his own zone of responsibility, and that the withholding of whatever was necessary for local success was evidence of blindness, if not imbecility, in the high command."[3]

Localitis is a complicated and sophisticated idea, going beyond the view that individual self-interest is the driving engine of organizational life. In describing localitis, George Marshall did not accuse local commanders of pursuing narrow, selfish interests. He emphasized their genuine conviction that their efforts were critical to winning the war.

Similarly, splintering forces arise because middle managers and functional heads believe that their work and their departments are critical to a company's success. Localitis originates with people who are well-intentioned, hardworking, and even self-sacrificing, but are simply captives of their own view of what their company really needs. Of course, self-interest often enters the picture. Added to localitis, it deepens the conflicts between people and units.

The Inertial Forces

Inertial forces in companies cause them to drift toward bureaucracy and inflexibility. The political philosophy assumes that people seek security and resist changes that make their lives uncertain or threaten their self-interests. Companies cope with this by resisting change, developing standard operating procedures (SOPs), and making decisions through "satisficing."[4]

Resistance to Change. Slow growth, competition from overseas, and intensified domestic competition resulting from overcapacity and deregulation have intensified pressures on managers. Rapidly evolving markets require companies to increase the pace at which they respond. But new strategies create uncertainties and threaten old skills and familiar ways of doing business—and the jobs of managers heavily vested in the status quo.

Resistance then sets in. People seek to reduce uncertainty through a variety of familiar practices. Rather than develop long-term strategies, they react to problems day-by-day. Rather than face the challenge, frustration, and anxiety of predicting uncertain future events, they "put out fires." They reduce uncertainty by adhering to conventional wisdom, following standard industry practices, and pursuing the satisfactory strategies and procedures of the past.

Standard Operating Procedures. A wide variety of standard operating procedures—which can be broadly defined as an organization's management system, and the formal and informal routines for making decisions—reduces uncertainty and makes it possible for people with different interests to get along. SOPs establish routines that help limit and shape the splintering political forces within a company. They also increase efficiency and help companies avoid reinventing the wheel for routine problems. SOPs guide and limit the ways in which managers seek solutions to problems. They determine who reports to whom, who receives what compensation, and how products, capital, and information flow through a company. They make it possible for critical activities to be performed reliably and consistently and also act as treaties or constitutions, defining the territories, rights, and duties of contending people and units.

However, systems and SOPs often become an inertial force of their own. They can suppress initiative and a sense of responsibility, giving rise to the attitudes "I am following orders"; It is not my fault"; "I can't do anything about it." And, even more bizarre, "The system made me do it." Systems can reach a Byzantine degree of elaboration and their further refinement can become an end in itself. Moreover, motivated by self-interest, some people will always find ways to beat even the most elaborate systems, consuming vital management time and creativity in the process.

Satisficing. "Satisficing" means that people and sub-units agree on responses that are "good enough." In finding ways of meeting market pressure, they focus on options that solve the immediate problem rather than strengthen a company's long-term competitive position. Satisficing occurs, in part, because people commonly try to solve new problems with approaches that worked for old ones. This saves time, effort, and thought, and does not threaten established practices or interests. Because problems tend to be categorized as "marketing," "manufacturing," or "financial," the search for solutions is often conducted within limited grounds. Satisficing often reflects the achievement of a delicate and complicated balance among the competing interests inside a company and among suppliers, customers, unions, and governments. If that balance has been difficult to achieve, reluctance to move away from it is rational.

Because people tend to satisfice, to avoid uncertainty, to react to problems rather than seek opportunities, and to use standard operating procedures, they often become motivated more by the need to move incrementally away from problems than by the desire to move toward goals. Unfortunately, the resulting decisions often lack an integrating strategic force.

The full impact of the inertial forces and the splintering forces is powerful and pervasive. But they need not destroy a company's competitive vitality. Strong leadership by a manager can harness them—but only if he or she is tough-minded in thinking about the forces and pragmatic in handling them.

THE PHILOSOPHY IN ACTION

These assumptions about the forces driving contemporary organizations have a single powerful implication: managers are as much captives as masters of their companies. They cannot lead by fiat. Instead, they must guide their companies so that the fragmented, dispersed efforts cumulatively reinforce company strategy, rather than derail it. But as companies become more complex, and as authority and responsibility are dispersed, managers have limited opportunities to act through direct, personal effort.

These are the realities of contemporary organizational life. To be effective, a leader must be a pragmatic realist who understands the degenerative forces and has the skills to modify and shape them in ways that motivate people to act in the interest of the company as a whole. Thus we come to the central tenet of political leadership: *strong business leaders must be adept at moving forward in small, incremental steps and at orchestrating astutely from behind the scenes.* Harvard Business School professor C. Roland Christensen, a long-time student of general management, makes this observation about the daunting task of bringing coherence to a company's many objectives:

> The uniqueness of a good manager lies in his ability to lead effectively organizations whose complexity he can never fully understand, where his capacity to control directly the human physical forces comprising that organization is severely limited, and where he must make or review and assume ultimate responsibility for present decisions which commit concretely major resources for a fluid and unknown future.[5]

Setting and Communicating Company Goals

Setting and communicating a company's goals and the strategy to achieve them is a manager's basic responsibility. According to the political view of leadership, companies are much more likely to enjoy outstanding performance if managers keep their goals general and flexible, and sometimes even vague. It is an illusion to think a company's strategy can be a systematic grand design based on detached, objective, rational analysis—or to believe company strategy can be captured in a comprehensive statement of goals and policies. Instead, strategy is a concept that evolves over time through administrative and political processes. Because of the political arenas inside companies and the uncertainties outside, adaptation must dominate analysis in developing company strategy. At any point, a company's strategy is best defined by the emerging pattern of its financial commitments and operating policies, along with many smaller, ostensibly nonstrategic decisions.

Of course, rational analysis plays a role in goal setting. But so do the power and preferences of important subunits and their managers, surprising opportunities and unexpected problems, modifications of information as it moves through the organization, and the timing of alternatives reaching top management. Because a detailed grand design cannot encompass all these factors, pragmatism rules.

Flexibility becomes critical. One reason is that a leader ultimately wants a genuine, strong consensus on a company's goals. But consensus rarely wells up naturally from within an organization. In fact, since strategic change can threaten the self-interest of many in an organization, the explicit statement of goals is bound to create resistance. Precise goals can become lightning rods and mobilize opposition to a leader's strategy. The communication of broad goals in more general terms minimizes the prospect that opposition to a leader's strategy will mobilize.

Consensus and teamwork must emerge from discussion, negotiation, give and take, and coalition building. Ralph Bailey summed it up this way:

> To maximize creativity and innovation among managers, you need to give them the full flexibility of generating all the new prospects and projects and ideas they can possibly come up with. They ought to be encouraged to do that. For that reason, ultimate goal setting should not

start from the top. To do that you would need a big broad hierarchy up there with the capacity to think about all these things and send them down into a pyramidal organization. Instead, the people near the marketplace and running the operations should be generating most of the new ideas.

It is much easier to achieve consensus around broad statements of objectives—such as becoming cost competitive or improving product quality—than around specific statements. Purely financial objectives—such as return on investment and earnings and growth targets—tend to be the least threatening and intrusive form of goals, since they leave subordinates considerable discretion in deciding how to achieve them.

Precise goals elaborated from the top also promote rigidity. Philip Knight, the founder and chairman of Nike, reflected on this:

> A plan is more than a list of where we are going to be: Point A, Point B, Point C. The problem is that the plan never works out in the way you thought it would. When we look ahead over the next three or four years and say, "Here's a plan with a capital P"—and we've done this a little bit—the guys in the middle read it and think it is cast in stone. Then the plan becomes a substitute for thinking. People stop thinking about why they are doing what they are doing. This leads to all kinds of bad decisions.[6]

Knight often illustrates his point with the story of the football team that was buried on its own five-yard line. To avoid the risk of a costly turnover, the coach gave the quarterback explicit instructions to run the fullback for two plays and punt on third down. The first two plays produced gains of forty-five and forty yards. On the third play, with the ball on the opponent's ten-yard line, the team punted.

Failure to be flexible, and sometimes ambiguous can

often damage morale and lead to outright unfairness. Looking back on thirty years of experience, Ralph Bailey commented:

> It's necessary to fix goals with a fair amount of flexibility in them, knowing that they are sure to change. You need to ensure that you set achievable goals, that others are going to be held accountable for them, and that you're going to hold yourself accountable for them. That means that a mentality is established that "we are going to do it." We will often set a corporate stretch target of, say, an additional $50 million in earnings, but won't assign them to a given unit. We convey the need to our managers and ask them to turn over every rock and look at every opportunity to help us do that. It is rare that we don't make our stretch targets. But if conditions change, we go back and reset the targets.

The rationale for broad, flexible goals extends beyond these internal factors. External pressures also demand flexibility. Outstanding performance requires that top management perform a continuous balancing act among the conflicting demands of labor unions, government agencies, and local communities and the demands of competitors and customers. This complicated task is difficult enough without the straitjacket of precise, detailed long-range plans.

There are also competitive reasons to surround goals in secrecy or to keep them vague. Detailed statements of goals can easily telegraph a management's strategy to its competition, derail ticklish negotiations, or undermine the morale of employees. In addition, uncertainty about the evolution of markets and government policy demands a flexible, incremental approach to goals. During periods of intense turbulence, precise goals can be counterproductive. Alexander d'Arbeloff put the issue this way:

> You've got a juggling act here, and you've got to keep it vague until you can see what's happening. What's happening is that you've got to react month-to-month. The

thing to do is keep the pressure on—for market share and for profits—so you can see which way this market is moving. If you became explicit now and you told people, here's your marching orders, you could be terribly wrong. You do it incrementally.

How does a manager communicate a strategy, if it is general and flexible? The answer is that a strategy is communicated over time, not at any one point in time. And it is communicated through a pattern of actions, not just through words. The pattern is shaped by a leader's own vision for the company, by opportunities that arise in an organization or the marketplace, and by the results of bargaining with subunit managers and external constituencies. In the end, only a pattern of decisions and commitments made over time clearly and accurately displays a company's strategy. What managers do counts far more than what they say.

At times, a strategy will not be known with perfect clarity throughout a company. This does not mean, however, that the strategy is just a vague notion in a leader's head. On the contrary, most outstanding leaders usually keep a few basic goals in mind. These act as a touchstone as they try to move their organizations incrementally forward. Here is a simple, persuasive summary of this incremental approach to setting company goals:

Von Clausewitz summed up what it had all been about in his classic *On War*. Men could not reduce strategy to a formula. Detailed planning necessarily failed, due to the inevitable frictions encountered: chance events, imperfections in execution, and the independent will of the opposition. Instead, the human elements were paramount: leadership, morale, and the almost instinctive savvy of the best generals.

The Prussian general staff, under the elder Von Moltke, perfected these concepts in practice. They did not expect a plan of operations to survive beyond the first contact with the enemy. They set only the broadest of objectives and emphasized seizing unforeseen opportunities as they arose. In current American parlance, the art of the broken field runner was the key to success. Strategy was not a lengthy action plan. It was the evolution of a central idea through continually changing circumstances.[7]

This perspective dramatically changes the role of top executives in developing strategy. They do not analyze and then announce. Instead, in a multitude of ways discussed later in this chapter, they manage the context in which other managers analyze information and make decisions and commitments.

Managing Formal Systems and Structures

The management systems and structures that make up the formal organization are powerful instruments for extending a manager's reach. They determine the allocation of formal authority and responsibility, route information, define how performance is measured and rewarded, and influence how and with whom managers spend their time. They determine how problems are defined and what solutions surface. Taken together, they create a complex pattern of transactions. In many respects, an organization can be viewed as a system for exchanging certain forms of work behavior for money, security, prestige, and power. In a well-managed company, the pattern of transactions is coherent: the structure and systems fit each other and both reinforce the strategy.

Systems and structures have political consequences. For example, a manager planning a major change in strategy may assign potential opponents to positions in which they will be too busy or too far from headquarters to mobilize resistance. In anticipation of a major, potentially controversial, strategic move, a politically astute manager will base promotion decisions on more than technical competence, and will assess the willingness of candidates to support his or her plans.

The formal organization also determines how intensely members of an organization will compete with each other and what the terms of their contest will be. Both Du Pont and IBM have, at times, created divisions with overlapping markets; as a result, two or more sales forces and manufacturing operations have competed for the same customers and the same pool of company resources. From a technical perspective, such redundancy is a mistake that should be corrected by analysis to determine which division is best equipped to serve which customers. From a political perspective, the competing units build competitive spirit and encourage the fullest exploitation of growing markets.

By the same token, corporate staffs are more than instruments that provide advice and assess performance. They expand the information base, and hence the power of senior executives. They are a channel through which senior executives can gently encourage actions they do not want to mandate directly, and they provide a way of floating trial balloons over uncertain political waters. An astute manager, keenly aware of the forces of self-interest and localitis, will build a formal organization that checks and balances these forces. This often entails the creation of staff units with the power to scrutinize information on prospective actions and demand explanations for past performance.

All leaders need accounting staffs to collect, analyze, condense, and communicate the financial information that allows them to keep a hand on the pulse of the organization, to identify problems, and to assess performance. But political leadership goes beyond this. Its adherents use staffs to check strategic plans, annual budgets, and capital appropriation requests for "political contamination." Often such a leader retains staffs of functional experts at the corporate level to evaluate the decisions of operating managers and recommend alternative courses of action. This staff capability extends the leader's ability to intervene to resolve problems that surface in operating units.

The wise executive manages changes in the formal organization very carefully. Major changes in systems and structures are far more likely to succeed if they are implemented with painstaking attention to the power and interests of those likely to be affected. For example, under Reginald Jones, General Electric pioneered many of the strategic planning systems common in U.S. companies today. Yet Jones spent nearly a decade putting these systems in place. In the early 1970s, he rejected a consulting firm's advice to replace GE's hierarchy of nearly 250 operating general managers with a new organization built around approximately forty strategic business unit (SBU) heads. Instead, he used the SBUs as a loose overlay on the existing organization and allowed the operating executives to tailor the SBUs to their needs. Through this strategy, Jones maintained operational control and avoided years of political infighting between representatives of the old and new systems. In the late 1970s, Jones seized an opportunity to invigorate the planning system by giving responsibility for different parts of it to the five candidates vying to succeed him as chairman. Naturally, they competed strongly to make the system work even better—and this gave other members of the company even stronger incentives to cooperate with GE's planning system.

Through patient, careful effort over nearly a decade, Jones evolved an approach to implementing strategic planning that addressed a central question of implementation: given its likely effect on the daily routines, positions, status, and power of key people and subunits, which approach looks most viable?

Resolving Conflicts

Managing and resolving conflicts is the third basic task of general managers. At critical times—when new products are introduced or when strategy changes—resources and power are up for grabs, misunderstandings about the intentions or expectations of others abound, differences in judgment can reach their greatest intensity, and older products, their managers, and the established ways of managing can be threatened. With the threats come resistance and internal conflict. At these times, political leadership is vital.

Political leaders attempt to avoid, or at least reduce, conflict by negotiating compromises. The alternatives—rancor, hostility, and, quite often, decisions by fiat—lead nowhere. Conflict only creates winners and losers who lock horns on other issues. And it drains time, thought, and emotion better devoted to running the business. Faced with potential conflict, a leader must consider questions like these:

Which of the compromises available in this situation will help others meet their personal or subunit needs in ways that move the organization closer to my long-term goals?

Which alternative is most likely to reduce conflict and defuse opposition to my objectives?

How can I save face for those who might lose in this situation?

If compromise is likely, what will I be willing to give up and what may I have to give up?

The manager who seeks a successful compromise must understand the stakes of the conflicting parties and the second-order consequences—the ripple effects—of alternative resolutions. A political leader needs considerable "soft" information on the values, personalities, and preferences of others. The leader must also be willing to forgo maximization of economic objectives and instead to choose approaches that gain support and minimize resistance, approaches that are satisfactory rather than optimal.

Success requires paying careful attention to the maxim, "the better is the enemy of the good." Successful leaders seek what works, not what is perfect. They are constantly on the lookout for "corridors of indifference" through which they can move toward their goals, without impinging on the self-interest of others or eliciting resistance.[8]

The need for negotiated compromise is not just internal. To reduce uncertainty, managers at times negotiate "contracts" with external constituencies to make the environment more predictable. The historic GM agreement with the UAW in 1948, nicknamed the "Treaty of Detroit," ended years of wildcat strikes, gave GM managers greater control over the workplace, and let them plan production and capacity much more confidently. In a similar vein, standard patterns of marketplace behavior and industry tradition make competitive rivalry more predictable. These "rules of the game" effectively are loose, tacit contracts among competitors.

One thing is clear: the need to compromise future plans to resolve present conflict (both internal and external) means the path to the leader's goals will rarely be direct. The bargains struck to resolve conflicts send powerful signals about future directions. They are part of the pattern of action that defines and communicates a company's strategy. People note carefully who appears to have won or lost and act accordingly. The bargains also determine, often in small increments, a company's competitive strengths and areas of vulnerability.

Managing Day by Day

How do general managers spend their days? The idealized professional manager does it this way:

> The professional manager in America exists above the industrial din, away from the dirt, noise, and irrationality of people and products. He dresses well. His secretary is alert and helpful. His office is as clean, quiet, and subdued as that of any other professional. He plans, organizes, and controls large enterprises in a calm, logical, dispassionate, and decisive manner. He surveys computer printouts, calculates profits and losses, buys and sells subsidiaries, and imposes systems for monitoring and motivating employees, applying a general body of rules to each special circumstance. The symbols in which he thinks and works are those of finance, law, accounting, and psychology.[9]

But in practice, management life is one of fragmentation and interruption. The trivial jostles the important in an endless series of meetings, memos, questions, and problems. Henry Mintzberg, in his important study of the daily activities of managers, described a multitude of brief encounters with others, fragmented schedules, and a stream of often ill-defined, diverse problems calling for solutions. He concluded:

> The variety of activities to be performed is great, and the lack of pattern among subsequent activities, with the trivial interspersed with the consequential, requires that the manager shift moods quickly and frequently. In general, managerial work is fragmented and interruptions are commonplace. Because of the open-ended nature of his job, the manager feels compelled to perform a great quantity of work at an unrelenting pace. . . . Superficiality is an occupational hazard of the manager's job.[10]

A constant in all this diversity is the scores of contacts managers have with other people. How do effective leaders approach these daily relations with others? A recent study addressed this question. John Kotter studied fifteen very successful general managers and found that they worked through

> . . . . an ongoing, largely incremental, largely informal process which involved a lot of questioning and produced a largely unwritten agenda of loosely connected goals and plans. . . . Agendas tended to cover a wider time frame than did most formal plans; they tended to be less numerical and more strategic in nature; they usually dealt more with "people " issues; and they were typically somewhat less rigorous, rational, logical, and linear in character.[11]

The upshot of these studies is clear. First, most managers work as much on process—on the ways in which people and groups make decisions and take action—as on the analytical, economic substance of the issues facing their company.

Second, they lend support to the political philosophy of leadership, namely that successful managers work with loose, flexible agendas, which they modify and improve incrementally.

A Nonthreatening Approach. The political philosophy of leadership gives a clear, commonsense way of building an agenda and managing process. It starts with the personal behavior of the leader. He or she must act in a nonthreatening way. This means avoiding the cool, analytical distance of the archetypal professional manager, or the demanding, sometimes punitive style of the manager as military leader.

A nonthreatening manner makes other people comfortable. Ralph Bailey described it in these terms:

> You have to present yourself as someone who is extremely interested, who wants to be more knowledgeable about what is going on, wants to learn about people as people. You have to show that you are warm and friendly and congenial. You have to invite their questions and make a very sincere effort to be responsive to them. You cannot march around in organizations speaking down to people. You've got to operate from their level as best you can and make them comfortable.

What are the benefits of behaving in this nonthreatening way? First, putting subordinates at ease helps managers hear vital, candid information, judgments, and even hunches about the politics and the substance of key issues. The more sources managers have and the more candid the sources are, the better they can get a fix on a situation by "triangulating"— seeking out and then sifting different views of the same situation. Second, managers get better answers to two critical questions: Do I have enough information from enough sources to assess the facts and politics of the situations I face? Who will support and who will oppose what I want to do?

The value of drawing on a broad range of candid comments cannot be overestimated. Marvin Bower, the managing director of McKinsey & Co. from 1950 to 1967, concluded: "The people who work in a company don't tell the boss very much. It's a fact of business life that the larger the corporation, the more awe the chief executive inspires, and the less information he gets from the inside."[12] No one wants to bring the boss bad news. Richard Munro emphasized the reality of this problem:

> I've been here for twenty-eight years, and I know damn near everybody in this building. And yet the minute I walked into the CEO's job, things were different. I could feel it. I could smell it. Nothing overt, but you get the impression that people do pull their punches. That they do not tell you, maybe, everything they should. Not everybody is perfectly secure in their jobs, even though we don't fire people around here. That's how the world works.

Informal Communications. By relying heavily on informal communications channels, managers can also reduce the need to make formal decisions. Informal channels can be used to send information as well as receive it—and with a low profile. By informally suggesting options, paths of analysis, or reconsiderations, managers can avoid tying themselves or their company to particular policies. They can suggest small moves or inexpensive experiments, get results quickly and informally, and then make further suggestions. All of this increases their flexibility.

Most difficult decisions directly affect the careers and self-images of many people. By relying on informal communications channels, leaders can also be much more sensitive in their dealings with others. What may appear to outsiders as politics or lack of courage is often a decision by a senior executive to act informally and privately out of consideration for an individual. Sensitivity and fairness—both subtle and elusive—are much harder to maintain through formal, public, official dealings that attract attention and set precedents. For example, at one *Fortune* 500 company, the CEO decided that two outspoken people would have to leave the company for concealing important information and insubordinate conduct. He did not fire them in a dramatic public move. Instead, he spoke with each of them, explained his conclusion, and asked them to resign. Later, even though others interpreted the departures as politics, the CEO stood by his decision to keep the matter private to protect the executives' reputations and future careers.

One of a political leader's most useful skills is the ability to ask perceptive questions. Indeed, insightful questions can be a substitute for orders. They place subordinates on notice that the issue in question has high visibility and that their responses, both in word and in action, may influence their superior's appraisal of them.

There are other, smaller ways in which the philosophy of political leadership guides daily management work. At meetings, leaders are careful not to signal their position prematurely, which would discourage others from expressing their views. Believing that strong personal feelings can cloud the judgments they must make, they are friendly, but rarely intimate with others in a company. They try to anticipate others' reactions and save face for them. When developments are not going as they want, they often passively resist or stall rather than issue orders.

Political leadership is a consistent approach to handling managers' problems and opportunities. It presupposes that a leader has a set of objectives that will, if achieved, move the company ahead and translate the leader's vision into reality. But a political leader's inclination is to view problems from an exceedingly practical perspective, asking:

What are the strategic objectives I should try to advance in this situation?

What is the political situation?

  Who favors or opposes particular alternatives?

  Who has what stakes in the resolution of the problem?

What are my alternatives?

  What sources of influence can I use to shape the problem's resolution?

  What compromises are feasible?

Which alternative is most likely to induce conflict and mobilize opposition to my objectives?

What are the possible "corridors of indifference" through which I could move?

Does the situation present an opportunity to shake up the organization in order to create more room for maneuver and new alternatives for action (through trial balloons, the use of organizational mavericks to test new ideas, and so forth)?

What is the most effective way to implement this decision?

How can I make the decision seem to be a win/win situation for the people who are critical to its implementation?

What set of participants, what agenda, and what setting will be most conducive to achieving my objectives?

What language can I use to avoid a premature commitment that would limit my future flexibility?

What can I do to ensure that the outcome is correctly interpreted when it passes through the organization?

If the outcome is not what I planned, are there ways in which I can impede or stall the undesirable outcome?

As shown by these questions, a political leader works on process and politics as much as the substance of issues. In the end, company strategy is the sum of a leader's vision, and a long series of negotiations, compromises, adjustments, and reactions to unanticipated opportunities and obstacles.

NOTES

1. For a discussion of power and its many organizational uses see John Kotter, *Power and Influence* (New York: Free Press, 1985); Henry Mintzberg, *Power In and Around Organizations* (Englewood Cliffs, NJ: Prentice-Hall, 1983); and Jeffrey Pfeffer, *Power in Organizations* (Boston: Pitman, 1981).
2. Richard R. Ellsworth, "Subordinate Financial Policy to Corporate Strategy," *Harvard Business Review*, November–December 1983, p. 175.
3. Arthur M. Schlesinger, Jr., *The Coming of the New Deal* (Boston: Houghton Mifflin, 1958), pp. 521–522.
4. The role of standard operating decisions and "satisficing" decision making in organizations is fully developed in the works of members of the

"Carnegie School." The most important of these are Herbert Simon, *Administrative Behavior* (3d ed. New York: Free Press, 1976), Richard Cyert and James March, *A Behavioral Theory of the Firm* (Englewood Cliffs, NJ: Prentice-Hall, 1963), and Simon and March, *Organizations* (New York: John Wiley, 1958).

5. C. Roland Christensen, "Education for the General Manager," (unpublished working paper, Harvard Business School).

6. David C. Rickert and C. Roland Christensen, "Nike" (C), 385-029. Boston: Harvard Business School, 1984, p. 9.

7. Kevin Peppard, Bendix Corporation, letter to *Fortune*, 30 November 1981, p. 17.

8. Chester I. Barnard in *The Functions of the Executive* used the term "zone of indifference," which he defined as the domain in which individuals will accept orders "without consciously questioning their authority." It is the area between support for a proposal and subtle resistance or outright opposition to it. See Chester I. Barnard, *The Functions of the Executive* (Cambridge, MA: Harvard University Press, 1938), p. 73.

9. Robert B. Reich, untitled book review, *The New Republic*, 27 June 1981, p. 27.

10. Henry Mintzberg, *The Nature of Managerial Work* (New York: Harper & Row, 1973), p. 51.

11. John P. Kotter, *The General Managers* (New York: Free Press, 1982), p. 126.

12. James E. Aisner, "A Premium on Scholarship," *Harvard Business School Bulletin*, February 1985, p. 62.

Chapter 2

DIRECTIVE LEADERSHIP

It doesn't bother me in the slightest to have someone
walk away saying, "My view prevailed," and someone
else saying, "My view didn't," as long as I let them
know why they didn't prevail. There isn't any way to
make everybody walk away feeling good about it. You
are soft-soaping people when you try to make them feel
good.

> Walter Wriston,
> former chairman, Citicorp

The way to lead an organization is to be a tire kicker.
You need to get out there where the field commanders
are and find out what is going on. I want to know not
only what we are doing, why we are doing it, and how
we are doing it, but even more important, who is doing
it.

> Ralph Bailey,
> former chairman, Conoco

Unlike political leadership, directive leadership
places overriding importance on facts, on the strategic substance of decisions, and on the direct, personal involvement of
the leader in guiding his or her company to superior performance. Outstanding general management involves directing a
company toward clear, specific, and compelling goals. These
goals are arrived at not by way of internal political demands
but through an objective assessment of the company's potential and an analysis of its competitive position.

To achieve exceptional company performance, a
leader must be direct, clear, and forceful in dealings with

others: directly confront internal conflicts; take personal responsibility for key decisions; challenge standard ways of operating within the company as well as the conventional wisdom of the industry and the capital markets; use systems and structure to provide clear direction to subordinates and secure greater control over the company's operations; and generate the best practical information for making decisions at all levels of an organization.

THE PHILOSOPHY OF DIRECTIVE LEADERSHIP

Directive leaders make three strong assumptions about people and organizations. First, people are motivated more by internal forces than by external prods. Second, organizations need strong pushes toward coherence. Third, coherence and substance are more important than style. In other words, action is better than reaction. These three beliefs combined have far-reaching implications for how organizations are managed and how leaders should act.

Personal Internal Forces Predominate

Narrowly defined self-interest alone does not motivate people. Talented people are motivated by more than concerns for security, power, status, and financial rewards. As Abraham Maslow and David McClelland both have observed, strong needs for achievement and self-fulfillment drive high-caliber people.[1] In companies people derive self-fulfillment in large part from achievement. The drive for achievement leads one to want personal responsibility for making decisions and the opportunity to "win" as a result of one's own efforts. The focus on achievement results in a desire for clear, concrete feedback on performance. (Money, in the form of salary and bonus or in unit profitability, can be one measure of achievement.) A well-managed company fulfills each of these desires.

In any company, a significant number of people are competitive. They are powerfully motivated by the challenge of participating on a winning team and the excitement of winning a competitive marketplace battle. Of course, this attitude does not come easily or naturally to everyone, but with proper encouragement, with the right environment, and with the right leadership, many people—far more than is commonly supposed—will rise to the competitive challenge. And when they do so, they will not be acting only in their own narrow self-interests. Their satisfaction will derive directly from the company's success, which in large part they will see as a mark of their own accomplishment.

Most people can accomplish feats beyond their ordinary expectations, but to reach their potential, people must be pressed, stretched, and inspired to meet ever higher standards. The reward for people is pride in their achievements; for the company it is exemplary competitive performance. Most talented people prefer to work in a meritocracy. That is, they want control over their work lives and activities, they want responsibility for important tasks, and they want to be rewarded for—which implies being held accountable for—their performance. They are willing to risk mediocre rewards, or even losing their jobs, if they don't meet expectations.

Business competition should be fun for those fully engaged in it. Leaders demonstrate the excitement of responding to the challenge of external competition. They believe that others should share this sense of fun and excitement—and their behavior tends to be infectious. The president of a major semiconductor manufacturer facing tough Japanese competition exemplified this feeling. He commented, "Sure, we expect a great deal of people. But if you are competitive, a tough race is a turn-on; an easy race is a bore."

The Push to Coherence

Organizations are indeed subject to strong splintering pressures, but it is the *lack* of leadership that causes subunits to drift. To overcome localitis, most organizations create ever more complex systems, structures, and controls. As a result, people and subunits adhere to rules, procedures, and strategies, especially those that have proved successful in the past. Unfortunately, when established techniques and operating procedures grow powerful, they limit creativity and imagination, causing organizations to degenerate into lumbering, politicized bureaucracies, vulnerable to competitive attack.

The operation and maintenance of complex systems often require staffs. If the staffs are composed of high-caliber people, it is only natural that they will try to expand their jurisdictions and to develop more services to offer line management. Strong, capable people, with the best of intentions but with a touch of localitis, will vigorously attempt to increase their influence. The consequence can be increased line-staff conflict and more complex decision making, which undermine the timeliness and quality of decisions.

Unless senior managers set a strong example, internal competition for resources, power, and prestige will overshadow external competitive battles. Time, energy, and funds will not be spent optimally. Careerism, rather than competitive considerations, will drive decisions. Political maneuvering will undermine trust and the perception of fairness throughout the organization. Consequently, talented people are driven away.

Trust also erodes, and so communication becomes less open. The information on which decisions are made and performance is evaluated becomes politically distorted, and managers find it harder to make informed decisions and secure the cooperation they need to implement strategy. When information is modified to serve political purposes and resolve petty conflicts, this seriously weakens people's commitment to a company's central purpose. A company's competitiveness can be seriously undermined by the effect of politicized information on morale and on people's ability to make strategic, rational decisions.

Internal politics are not, however, the inevitable result of organized activity. Through forceful, vigilant action and strong example, managers can attack and subdue the political maneuvering that frustrates internal cooperation and diverts time and resources from the central task of building a sustainable competitive advantage.

Through continually pressing for personal achievement, a leader bonds followers to an organization and its purpose.

Substance before Style

Managers should not adapt their mode of leadership to fit the motivations of the people who represent the common denominator of society. If the recruitment and development processes are working effectively—and it is a principal responsibility of leadership to see that they do—then all levels of the organization should have people with talent and initiative who want to work in *that* company.

Ideas, well-conceived and clearly articulated, have considerable power in directing the behavior and commitment of people toward issues of substance. Competition and excellent performance turn on substance. Linking accomplishment, motivation, and ideas to create an internal marketplace in which the best ideas ultimately prevail shapes the motivations of employees, the quality of company decisions, and, consequently, its performance.

THE PHILOSOPHY IN ACTION

Directive leaders and political leaders provide fundamentally different answers to the question of how general managers should meet some of their basic responsibilities, namely developing strategy, managing formal systems and structures, resolving conflict, and managing day by day.

Setting and Communicating Company Goals

Rather than merely responding to opportunities subordinates generate, a leader acts. He or she uses judgment, imagination, and insight to develop a vision of what the company can become and how it can be more competitive. The leader embeds this vision, which has both intellectual and emotional roots, in a clear concept of the company's mission and in a set of goals and policies that are clearly and precisely communicated.

Benjamin Disraeli once observed, "The secret of success is constancy of purpose." A leader's deep commitment to a company's purpose and his or her direct, forceful communication of strategy provide a constancy that can profoundly affect the company's performance. The company's purpose then reflects a personal quest and intense, sometimes obsessive dedication. Furthermore, if leaders are consistent in word and deed, others know where they stand on critical issues.

Walter Wriston, credited with dramatically reshaping Citibank and the banking industry, saw this clear definition of mission and constancy in its pursuit as the most critical aspect of good leadership:

> You have to have a vision of what you want to do and a clear set of well-articulated goals. Corporate statements of mission are either a bubble-gum wrapper or they are real. Ours was a real mouthful. We were a bank with a few foreign branches that were not doing all that well. So we said that we are going to be a "global financial intermediary." Three words—what the hell do they mean? Being a global financial intermediary is as different as night and day from being just a bank with foreign branches. Saying that changes other people's thinking. For example, some bright person then comes up and says, we have to be in the merchant banking business. If you really know what business you're in, then a lot of the rest flows from that. The mission is the framework.

A leader's vision permeates a company's goals and policies. Based on competitive realities, not financial abstractions, goals should be tightly linked to customer needs and competitor reactions. The consequence is a focus on precise strategic objectives that serve the customer, blunt competitors' moves, and seize opportunities—not on financial goals with their inherent vagueness and tendency to emphasize improving on last year's numbers.

Managerial actions should guide the company's strategy. If corporate management does not define a company's goals, people at lower echelons will. Conflicting objectives that undermine performance and morale and politicize the organization could be the result.

Why is it important for a leader to be actively involved in the analysis and creative thinking essential to a sound strategy? This involvement helps ensure that goals and policies reflect a thorough, systematic assessment of the company's competitive, social, and political environment. By challenging conventional wisdom and industry norms, and encouraging subordinates to do likewise, a manager can also instill an innovative spirit in an organization. Leaders should seed their own ideas and encourage others' ideas. As one CEO put it, "To move the company the way you want to go, you have to put an idea in the market and it has to be purchased." For ideas to be "purchased," they must be clear and well founded. In addition, listening to others' ideas is critical—"most good ideas come from someone other than the CEO."

Encouraging others to participate in discussion, analysis, and decisions does not mean managing by consensus or abdicating authority. Companies are not democracies. When tough decisions must be made, "consensus management" can delay decision making and threaten decisive action with compromise. Outstanding managers confront conflict and avoid compromising on critical issues simply to achieve consensus. Unwilling to wait for consensus to arise, they listen, persuade, and then, if necessary, command.

This does not mean that directive leaders do not value cooperation. On the contrary, they prize internal cooperation as a way to secure competitive advantage in the marketplace. But true cooperation comes from commitment to common objectives in an organization that values an open, objective, and fair exchange of ideas on substantive issues. Hence, subordinates must know that they will have their "day in court." Walter Wriston stressed the importance of giving priority to ideas over maneuvers to achieve consensus:

> The power of the ideas is what works. You aren't going to be able to build consensus first thing in the morning.

But if the idea is right, people will eventually perceive it as being right. Smart people have to be persuaded that what you are doing is reasonable. That is when consensus comes.

As a result of the power of objective analysis to motivate decisions, consensus often develops after a decision is made. But consensus is not a manager's objective, performance is. The best way to get superior performance is through putting forth ideas, hashing them out, and having open debate on their merits.

Objectivity is a critical part of developing strategy. Alfred Sloan attributed an important part of General Motors' success to the creation of an organization that focused on facts:

> An essential aspect of our management philosophy is the factual approach to business judgment. The final act of business judgment is of course intuitive. Perhaps there are formal ways of improving the logic of business strategy, or policy making. But the big work behind business judgment is in finding and acknowledging the facts and circumstances concerning technology, the market, and the like in their continuously changing forms. . . .
>
> In the corporation there is an atmosphere of objectivity and enjoyment of enterprise. One of the corporation's great strengths is that it was designed to be an objective organization, as distinguished from the type that gets lost in the subjectivity of personalities. . . .
>
> It is imperative for the health of the organization that it always tends to rise above subjectivity.[2]

Ultimately, however, analysis runs up against its limits. Analysis can improve decision making, foster objectivity, and focus attention on issues of substance, but it is handicapped in dealing with strategic issues. Strategy deals with the future, and there are few facts about the future. The formulation of strategy requires a manager to exercise judgment. Repeatedly, the leaders we interviewed made references to "a feeling in my stomach," "a gut feel," "a visceral feeling." For example, Walter Wriston commented:

> Make sure you get the best people you can, keep them as accountable as you can, quantify everything that is quantifiable, be as professional as anyone can possibly be—but when the big decisions come, go with your gut. Forget all that other crap. When you look at people's success in this corporation, it usually is made up of a series of very important decisions that were motivated by a deep conviction that they were right when a lot of people said they were wrong.

Communication Tools. To communicate their strategic objectives clearly and explicitly, leaders should use the full range of opportunities available to them: words, actions, decisions, systems, and structures. Hands-on involvement and enthusiastic enforcement of high standards make the meaning of personal commitment and the desired actions clear to subordinates.

Focus on a Few Objectives. Setting high standards that focus on one or a very few principal objectives critical to creating and maintaining a competitive advantage is very important. Leaders don't have time to be everywhere in their organizations, but they want their goals to be clearly understood and to influence decisions and behavior throughout a company. Power is amplified when what they say and do concentrates on a few clear, fundamental objectives. Moreover, if everybody knows what a leader wants done, it is much more difficult to engage in political maneuvering. One leader put it this way, "I try to have a few things, never more than three, that I'm driving on myself."

In today's complex organizations, one person can no longer be the sole repository of leadership. Leaders should play the role of a demanding coach, concentrating on the fundamentals. This was the role that Archie McCardell played in his early years at International Harvester, when he significantly improved the company's performance. After rejecting a 1978 budget which had been months in preparation, McCardell created a small policy committee made up of Harvester's group presidents which, with his detailed leadership, discussed strategic plans, cost reduction, performance against competitors, and financial results—all in detail. One participant commented later that the sessions communicated "very effectively that the boss really cared that we got a handle on a given problem."

Throughout these sessions McCardell concentrated on one fundamental that he phrased as getting Harvester to be "as good as the best within five years." To achieve this objective during his first two years as CEO, he single-mindedly stressed cost reduction. "Our biggest problem was to learn to focus on one issue and follow through on it. We started with the cost issue." In two years, Harvester did close the gap between itself and its competitors—GM, Ford, Caterpillar, and John Deere—significantly. Although Harvester's progress was derailed by the confluence of a record strike, record interest rates, and an economic recession that brought Harvester near bankruptcy, McCardell's example is a clear one. Leaders focus on monitoring, controlling, and directing a few critical aspects of a company's operations: goals, key functional policies, major commitments of resources, and the selection, development, and placement of key personnel.

Jack Welch, the CEO of General Electric, has also focused on a few objectives and has set high standards. Even for a company as diversified as GE, Welch argued that a CEO must "set an objective, one central theme to run through every bone in the company, every corner of it, every person in it." The direction he has chosen for GE is that each business should position itself to be number one or number two in its industry over the long term. From this objective come the themes of excellence, quality, and innovation—a desire to make GE "the most entrepreneurial large company in the world"—as well as candor and openness.[3]

Broad financial objectives alone won't do. Because precise goals often spark internal resistance, strategies should be translated into a detailed set of targets relating to competitiveness—such as market share, product innovation, cost reduction, customer service, and quality control goals. Goals that are linked to customer needs and performance in product markets keep subordinates focused on external competitive performance and not on internal battles for power.

It is one thing to have a vision, another to put it into action. The ability to envision "how things might be" would be of limited value without the courage to act. Even in the face of considerable uncertainty and disappointing setbacks, leaders work with dogged persistence to translate visions into goals, goals into plans, and plans into action. Consequently, directive leaders are often seen as tough, demanding taskmasters who tenaciously follow up on subordinates' progress in implementing key plans and who consistently reinforce the company's goals.

Clarity and Focus. The more precise and focused the goals are, the greater is their power to direct employees' actions, secure their commitment to corporate objectives, and focus a company's resources on some unique and sustainable competitive advantage. Clear, focused goals are especially important when top management wants to push forward with a major thrust, particularly if it differs from what a company has done before or if a crisis has caused the organization to seek new direction.

First, most employees prefer clear direction to vague goals, negotiation, and compromise. In an increasingly complex organizational and competitive environment, clear direction reduces ambiguity and uncertainty, which can produce anxiety. Second, clear goals make it easier for a company's executives to evaluate plans and decisions and to assess whether particular activities move the company closer to achieving its long-term goals. The more detailed and specific the goals are, the clearer it is whether a particular activity will contribute to their achievement. The activity can then be pursued or dropped. Third, definite expectations simplify and guide subordinates' approaches to problems and decisions, communicating priorities in decision making. Finally, the more specific the standards of performance are, the more likely it is that these standards will be perceived as fair, and the clearer is the link between the economic self-interests of individual employees and their company.

Managing Formal Systems and Structures

Organizational practices and processes easily become ends in themselves—or lead managers to act as if they were. For example, for several years, a California-based business unit of a large firm failed to achieve its recognized growth potential. In fact, it lost market share because its managers were rewarded almost exclusively for making quarterly profit numbers. This measure of performance did not make sense for the California market, but the parent company used it across the board. Thus, standard practices triumphed over the strategic logic of the individual business.

This should not happen. Systems and structures are only *means* for achieving a company's aims and amplifying the leader's strategic vision, not ends in themselves. Alexander d'Arbeloff commented, "Almost all strategic insights have nothing to do with process. Process mainly has to do with their dissemination."

For E. H. "Hubie" Clark, Jr., who, as CEO of Baker International, built an assemblage of small oil field service firms into one of the most successful companies of the 1970s, the process of strategic planning was secondary to the substance of the plan. He observed that simplicity and focus in the process facilitate the creation of a sound strategy:

> The greatest purpose of planning is not to create the plan but to tell the manager what he should be doing with his time. The plan is not important. What is important is that the people who make the plan know what they must do. Every time we make a plan, each divisional chief ex-

ecutive must report to the group president the five most important things he must do to make the plan happen.

Systems and structures are devices for getting information and resources to the people who need them so they can make sound decisions and coordinate efforts. Systems and structures also provide leaders with the information they need to set objectives, assess performance, and make critical decisions.

Outstanding general managers must have extraordinary competence, functional expertise, and the ability to identify, analyze, and resolve complex problems that require a coordinated response across several functional areas. It is important to leverage these capabilities as much as possible. Systems and structures enable managers to apply their skills more widely, and to extend their personal influence and control over more of the organization. Compensation systems, resource allocation systems, planning and control systems, management development programs, and formal organizational structures can all enhance a leader's efforts to directly influence behavior and to guide an organization in desired directions.

As useful as these systems are, however, they are only blunt instruments. They cannot provide clear enough direction and often lead to unintended consequences. Thus managers must reinforce management systems with their own direct, forceful, and consistent words and actions.

Autonomy versus Control. How a leader manages systems often has greater impact on a company than the formal mechanics of the systems themselves. When size, diversity, complexity, or other pressures limit a manager's ability to become directly involved in situations, a manager has two broad options: build up staff to gather and evaluate more information and to check on line managers' decisions, or increase the autonomy granted to others and rely on them to take appropriate action with limited staff scrutiny. The latter course is the only way to develop other managers into leaders. This approach can lead to a diffusion of power, but out of this diffusion can come a surge of leadership throughout a company. In this context, structures and systems serve two purposes. They communicate and reinforce the objectives, assumptions, and criteria on which other managers make decisions. And they ensure that these managers get the information, resources, co-operation, and freedom from bureaucratic meddling that they need.

Simplicity.   Structures and systems should be kept simple for several powerful reasons. First, leaders can become directly involved in decisions. With buffers and filters between themselves and operations removed, they get a direct, upward flow of information from the marketplace. Alexander d'Arbeloff, who stressed the fundamental importance of having a feel for the market, observed: "The sense of where the market is going needs to be a very personal one. This is difficult to achieve by working through a staff."

Second, simple organizations do not ensnarl and frustrate operating managers with bureaucratic procedures. With minimal staffs, line managers have much more control over their decisions. Since they are closer to the market, they can make decisions much more rapidly. In this way, simplicity helps all the managers in a company work directly and personally on problems, not just the CEO. Simple structures and systems are less likely to send convoluted or erroneous signals, which could result in unintended consequences.

The more complex and ornate the systems, the more likely they are to become empty rituals or political tools that distort information and prevent sound decisions. The ritualistic use of systems can arise from the natural tendency to avoid personal criticisms of others' judgments. When this occurs, the systems no longer facilitate the airing of important, controversial issues. Instead, they merely provide a vehicle for people to go through the motions of "thorough analysis and review" of difficult problems. This may provide the easy gratification of routine work and also soothe the conscience, but it strips the decision-making process of much of its substance. Even under the guidance of a strong leader, formal planning review meetings can lack substance.

When the process becomes more important than the facts, procedural issues sap management's energies, deflect attention from the substance of key decisions, and severely reduce a company's flexibility to respond to opportunities or competitive threats. Leaders need to be on constant vigil to eliminate ritual, minimize the political contamination of information, and focus discussions on substance. Jack Welch of General Electric once found himself at a business meeting that had deteriorated into what he called a "Mexican hat dance," an exercise in which everybody knew what the problems were but no one would say anything explicitly about them. He stopped the meeting and said, "We all know the problem, now what's in our bodies that we can't talk about the problem?" He later observed: "That was a nice way for all of us to have about a half an hour of guys just unloading. It was a good discussion though, it was a healthy discussion, because that is something that you don't talk about in these types of meetings."[4]

Welch faced a challenge when he took over as CEO of General Electric, a company long vaunted for its superb professional management and leadership in developing new management techniques. Welch had to take strong action to reduce planning rituals, which had begun to debilitate the company's strategic decision-making processes. He observed that the planning meetings had deteriorated so much that "you might as well have had robes and incense." In response, he dramatically cut the number of people attending the plan review meetings. Largely by personal example, he increased the openness of communication and the amount of disagreement that took place during meetings at which important decisions were made. He explained what happened:

[Our planning system] was dynamite when we first put it in. The thinking was fresh; the form was little—the format got no points—it was idea-oriented. Then we hired a head of planning and he hired two vice presidents, and then he hired a planner. Then the books got thicker, the printing got more sophisticated, the covers got harder and the drawings got better. The meetings kept getting larger. Nobody can say anything with 16 or 18 people there. . . .

So one of the things we have put into place is a way to achieve more candor, more constructive conflict. We've switched to meetings where the three of us [the chairman and the two vice chairmen] have meetings with SBU managers, one on three, in a small room.[5]

Resolving Conflict

A manager pays a price for compatibility; often the price is the truth. An emphasis on facts, substance, and open communication can raise hackles and create risk for some, but it discourages superficial, and sometimes dangerous, consensus. Discussion—even conflict—about the best way to achieve the company's goals must be encouraged.

Open and frank exchanges of ideas are essential to sound decision making and corporate morale. But openness and candor require that conflict be tolerated, even encouraged. As long as discussions are substantive—not driven by personal or subunit agendas—and as long as the discussions presuppose agreement with the leader's vision, disagreement and conflict are healthy. Such discussions can help develop wider ranges of alternatives and a better understanding of the strengths and weaknesses of each alternative. Walter Wriston summed it up this way:

We got into terrible arguments and debates, although we never got to the point of yelling and screaming at each other. If you have a group of smart people working their tails off, you are going to get dissension. That's healthy as long as it is based on a decent respect for each other's opinions.

When political maneuvering dominates, however, or when major disagreements arise over the company's fundamental direction, the dissidents should be forcefully brought around, isolated, or removed.

One executive said: "I'm open and my partner was open. There were a lot of arguments between us. We set the example. Culture is set by example, and open exchange is now part of our culture." Another leader described a meeting that took place shortly after his exceptionally successful company had been merged with another company. In meeting with the parent company's CEO and COO, he proposed that his company embark on a diversification program, which would use its packaged goods and technological know-how to benefit the parent. The COO sharply challenged the proposal. He argued that the acquired company's management should stick to managing the rapid growth of its existing business and attempt to increase its return on investment. As the debate became heated, the chief financial officer joined the discussion. He attempted to play the peacemaker by interjecting, "I think you guys are saying the same thing in different ways." The leader we interviewed retorted, "Thanks a million, but that isn't the case at all—we are having a basic disagreement. It's perfectly permissible. Thanks for the try." And the argument continued.

Some people do not like clear messages because they find their personal stakes jeopardized. These win-lose situations are unfortunate, but as this comment by Ralph Bailey shows, what matters above all is getting the outcome right:

> You don't want these things to linger on. It is debilitating to have unanswered questions or decisions left unmade. People will continue to spend time on the issue instead of doing what they should be doing. You want them to get on with the work at hand. For example, if someone is told, "We're not going to do it at this time" when you really mean, "We aren't going to do it ever," he'll go back and work more on the project. It is a waste of time. He ought to get a "yes" or "no." If you have reservations, tell him what they are so he can go back and improve it next time around. Fuzzy decisions are confusing to people.

Internal Cooperation and External Competition. Because they create an environment in which "the squeaky wheel gets the grease," continual negotiations to avoid conflict actually encourage undue internal competition and political maneuvering. Internal competition is acceptable if it is fair, if it deals with ideas, markets, and performance, rather than personality, and if everyone commits to the final decision. A company's central task is to outperform its competition. To do this, a company must have internal conflict so that the best ideas eventually win out and become part of the company's strategy. But once the internal contest is over and the strategy is settled, everyone must pull together.

Some companies, such as IBM, have institutionalized the process by which conflict is fostered and resolved. At IBM any plan must survive a "contention system" to be approved. All divisional plans are circulated to corporate staffs and to other operating units that have a stake in the plan. Corporate staffs must recommend approval or disapproval of the plan ("concur" or "nonconcur," in IBM parlance) by the Corporate Management Committee (CMC). The other operating units have the right to nonconcur if their interests are not being met or are in conflict with the plans of a given unit. In most cases, conflicting units resolve their nonconcurrences bilaterally. Those that are not are decided in the CMC. However, as one executive observed, "Neither side wants to lose, and you have that exposure whenever you go to the CMC for a decision."[6]

On occasions, however, staff units issue nonconcurrences to expose an important, but unstated, assumption to the CMC. A staff executive explained, "We have even taken issues to the CMC knowing we would almost certainly lose. We wanted to make sure that top management was conscious of all the aspects of the decision they were making. You want to be right, but sometimes there is value in making sure corporate management is aware there are alternative views."[7]

An emphasis on confrontation and openness requires taking a realistic approach to mistakes. If top management has been kept informed about problems along the way, people shouldn't be penalized for making mistakes based on well-conceived plans. Alexander d'Arbeloff summed up this approach:

> If somebody makes a mistake, we don't make much of a fuss about it. But if he didn't tell us, tried to hold the cards close to his vest, and wasn't really open about what was going on, we make a big fuss about it. We'll say, "We should have known about that. There should have been an open exchange. What the hell happened?"

Managing Day by Day

One of the most effective means of managing as well as developing managers is through day-by-day working relationships. Being articulate and listening avidly make the most of this means of influence.

Direct communication through personal contact aids a leader in the constant struggle to provide clear direction to a company, set high ethical and competitive standards, and combat localitis, overreliance on standard operating procedures, and the other splintering and inertial forces within companies. Direct contact is less likely to be misinterpreted than messages conveyed indirectly through management systems or staffs. Consequently, time spent in the field with operating managers yields great dividends. Ralph Bailey commented:

> I can get a totally different impression reading a report than if I go talk to the manager. Also, getting out there and seeing it with my own eyes increases my credibility with others in the organization. They know when I bring something up that it's not coming from someone who won't get out of the ivory tower or who thinks he has the wisdom to make judgments based on reports or staff recommendations.

Even Harold Geneen, the former chairman of ITT, who has been criticized for an overly formal approach to management, has declared that "facts from paper are not the same as facts from people." Direct contact also increases a leader's access to unfiltered information, which can be critical in making effective judgments. In addition, personal contact enables a leader not only to develop and express empathy for the needs of subordinates but to act quickly to suppress politicking.

Hiring and Developing Managerial Talent.   All outstanding general managers place great emphasis on hiring, developing, and promoting key personnel. The "people side" of the business is their single most important responsibility. Considerable time must be spent tracking the careers of key employees and ensuring that others in the organization are sensitive to the development of their managerial skills. GE's Jack Welch is a good example:

> I believe that it all starts with people. Put somebody in
> the job, let him or her develop a strategy, and then it
> goes from there. You don't start with strategy and then
> appoint somebody to execute it. It's the other way
> around. We are always trying to develop leaders who can
> create a strategic vision of their business, communicate
> it, and then lead its implementation.[8]

In the words of Alexander d'Arbeloff, "If you have the right person in the right spot, there is almost no way you can get hurt. If you have the wrong person, there is no way you can win."

All outstanding executives look for certain traits in their recruits: drive, competence, and enthusiasm. But other traits are also important: people should be candid or even blunt, have the courage to speak out on important issues, and be aggressive. However, while mavericks and people with strong determination challenge conventional wisdom— "shake the box"—and encourage independent thinking, a leader needs to directly channel the maverick's actions to prevent the "loose cannon" from smashing the ship.

Leaders should demand continual, precise, detailed evaluation of subordinates. For example, Citibank under Wriston had quarterly personnel review meetings at which pictures were hung on the wall of the 200 people considered to be the most capable in the company. These people were considered "corporate property"—no manager could block their progress if a more challenging opportunity opened up in another part of Citibank. The CEO and COO reviewed each of these individuals with their managers.

The Focused Taskmaster. Once a leader has communicated his or her objectives and put simple management systems in place, he or she needs to become a taskmaster. This means setting demanding standards and persistently following up on subordinates' efforts to meet them. While most people seek security and certainty, they also want outlets for their creativity and freedom from arbitrary interference in their lives. The leader must help subordinates reconcile the tension between their desire for security and their desire to take initiative. This is not accomplished by being paternalistic or by autocratically telling others what to do. Rather, it is done by driving people to accomplish more than they thought possible and giving them enough autonomy to put their personal mark on what they do. In doing a difficult job well, a person gains a greater sense of self-worth from his or her work.

No one should underestimate the power of competitive spirit: it justifies high standards, consistently enforced. Consider these comments from the leaders of three very successful companies:

We are never satisfied here. That's the way we are built. We always want to do better.

As a company grows larger and larger, one of the problems is how to maintain a high level of enthusiasm, determination, and willingness to work rather than have people relax and become mediocre. I don't want to be average. I think the average company is in a sorry state. You have to be way above average to make it in this free-enterprise system. People like to be stretched as long as the stretch is for the right reason and is reasonably done. It's the competitive spirit. It's why do you do thirty pushups instead of twenty-five. I think we really like to push ourselves and see what we can really achieve.

Competition is the foundation of man's development. It has made the human race what it is. It is the spur that makes progress. . . . Competition determines who will be the leader. It is the only known way that leadership and progress can be developed, if history means anything. It is a hard taskmaster. It is completely necessary for any-one—be he worker, user, distributor, or boss—if he is to grow. . . . Excellence brings rewards, self-esteem, respect.[9]

It is inevitable that some could see a driving, compet-itive leader as a tyrant. Consequently, fair play must temper toughness. Consistency, commitment to company purpose, fair enforcement of clear performance standards, openness to others' ideas, and emphasis on candor and substance, all re-duce this risk.

By personal example and direct action, leaders should ensure that the company operates as a meritocracy. Employees must be moved aside or fired if they lack the com-petence or commitment necessary to achieve excellence in the pursuit of common objectives. Morale suffers if chronic under-performers are treated in the same way as the achievers. For similar reasons, leaders may find it necessary to fire political maneuverers or people who resist a company's strategy once it is settled.

Fairness to the company matters as much as fairness to a person, and it is often fairer to both if misfits are fired sooner rather than later. Hubie Clark expressed it this way: "When it is clear that the division has outgrown a person's managerial abilities, the 'salvage operation' involved in retain-ing him is very high risk for everyone, including the person." Ralph Bailey commented, "When we see an imperfection in a manager, if he is acting out of self-interest, we usually find a way to sit down and discuss it with him. If that doesn't change things, we usually find a way to send him over to work for the competition."

In a meritocracy that emphasizes individual initiative, people deserve to be rewarded for what they contribute to a company's performance. Merit should determine who gets what, not benevolence granted from on high. Alexander d'Arbeloff summed up this view:

The company can't be paternalistic. Paternalism implies that the company knows what's best for everyone.
They don't want their employer coming down from the hill once a year to give them a Christmas turkey or to press a coin into their hand.

While being a taskmaster helps achieve high standards, this role carries the responsibility of helping subordinates achieve demanding objectives. Being responsible for clearly communicating the company's strategy and overseeing its implementation means that the leader *also* shares responsibility for the outcome. Repeatedly, the idea of a "co-mistake" surfaced in our interviews. One leader quoted the Yiddish saying, "The fish stinks from its head." He continued, "Since we do things jointly here, who do you blame when there is a mistake?" Hubie Clark summarized the views of many of the CEOs we interviewed:

It's most important that a person and his boss are together on what they should be doing. A boss has the obligation to use his experience to help. If someone is about to put his foot in a bucket and the boss doesn't see it, they are making a co-mistake. When it comes time to lay the lash, the boss is going to be more tolerant and fair.

In personal contacts with others, it is vital to set an example of open and direct communication, disdain for political maneuvering, and preoccupation with substance and facts rather than process. By listening, inviting questions, and responding directly, a leader shows respect for others' opinions and for an open, two-way exchange of ideas.
Subordinates who tend to say the politic rather than

the factually correct thing should be reprimanded clearly. One CEO was emphatic about politically motivated behavior:

> If anyone starts in on another person around here with-out invitation, I take his head off. I'll say, "It's none of your business! Crawl back in your hole! Mind your own goddamn business! If I'm interested in any input on that, I'll ask you. Why did you bring to the meeting a thing that affected his area that he hadn't seen before? What are you thinking about?"

He stated his reasons for this blunt, forceful position:

> When you have one of those cancers, you've simply got to go in and cut it out. If you can get these guys to-gether to talk the problem out, fine. If you can't, then I tell the two individuals, "You come down here. You and you are getting even with each other at the shareholders' expense. Why? If you can't work things out, I don't want anything to do with you."

As these comments indicate, forceful, vigilant action and strong example are needed to attack the political maneu-vering that frustrates internal cooperation and that diverts time and resources from the central task of building a strong competitive position.

This does not mean ignoring political realities. On the contrary, leaders should keep well informed of people's stakes in situations through personal contact and by asking key questions. But it is wrong to play politics or reward people who do play politics by compromising with them. Instead, localitis should be countered with a strong focus on facts and substance and, if need be, by harsh discipline of chronic "politicians."

Richard Munro described the climate within his com-pany in the following way. "If you come into this company thinking you can step on people to get ahead and that you can play the political game, the corporation will devour you. It will act like piranha: someday, you'll find yourself in eight million little pieces on the floor, and you won't know what happened to you. But you will not succeed here."

The same standards must apply to leaders as apply to their followers. One CEO adamantly stated, "A good leader avoids managing for his own self-interest like the plague. You never want to take an action simply because it fits your own self-interest better, rather than what is in the best interest of the organization. People are always looking for signals that you are not a 100 percent player."

When a leader is a taskmaster, is deeply committed to company goals and performance, and expects others to share his or her commitment, other people either love or hate him or her. People may join or leave a company because of these personal reactions.

Because of this self-selection, employees and managers often share traits and basic beliefs with their leaders. This offers a distinct advantage. When limited time and energy restrict the situations in which a leader can be directly involved and personally effective, leaders know they must depend on others to amplify, reinforce, and extend their influence. They need people who will act in their stead.

These day-by-day efforts all reinforce the central tenets of directive leadership. To excel, a manager must direct an organization clearly and forcefully toward his or her vision. According to this philosophy, leadership requires above all unremitting personal determination and direct, personal action.

NOTES

1. See Abraham H. Maslow, *Motivation and Personality* (New York: Harper & Row, 1954) and David McClelland, *The Achieving Society* (New York: Van Nostrand, 1961).
2. Alfred P. Sloan, Jr., *My Years with General Motors* (New York: Anchor Books, 1972), pp. xvi–xvii.

3. Presentation by John F. Welch at the Harvard Business School on 4 December 1981.
4. Presentation by John F. Welch at the Harvard Business School, 27 April 1981.
5. Ibid.
6. R. F. Vancil, *Implementing Strategy: The Role of Top Management* (Boston: Division of Research, Harvard Business School, 1981), pp. 43–45.
7. Ibid.
8. "A Conversation with John F. Welch, Jr., chairman and CEO, General Electric Company," *Outlook* (Booz, Allen & Hamilton, Inc., No. 9, 1985), p. 5.
9. Norman Berg and Norman Fast, "The Lincoln Electric Company," 376-028. Boston: Harvard Business School, 1975, pp. 3–4.

Chapter 3

VALUES-DRIVEN LEADERSHIP

The managerial life is the broadest, the most demanding, by all odds the most comprehensive and the most subtle of all human activities. And the most crucial. . . . [A manager's function] is to lead and move and bring out the latent capabilities—and dreams—of other human beings.[1]

> David E. Lilienthal, former chairman,
> Tennessee Valley Authority

If you have a culture that is clear about the tenets of your value system—integrity, fairness, honesty, and so forth—then the way the guy manages is his problem as long as he doesn't violate the culture.

> Walter Wriston, former chairman,
> Citicorp

Values are one thing you should not be flexible on. We do not temporize about morality with our people.

> James E. Burke, chairman
> of Johnson & Johnson

Exceptional company performance ultimately rests on the dedication and creativity of the entire organization. It does not stem solely from the subtle orchestration or intense personal direction of individual leaders. While such views of leadership do capture part of the truth, they are incomplete. Leadership means shaping an organization so that its values, norms, and ideals appeal strongly to its individual members while at the same time making the company a stronger competitor. When this occurs, outstanding performance follows.

THE PHILOSOPHY OF VALUES-DRIVEN LEADERSHIP

This philosophy of leadership is not simply an alternative to the other two. Rather, it transcends both of them. Certainly, organizations have political dimensions of which leaders must be aware, and localitis and political jockeying must not overshadow substantive issues and dominate managers' thinking and behavior. But direct, personal involvement is not enough. A leader's actions must serve purposes and reflect basic values that followers identify with personally. Followers must become committed to their organizations instead of to their leaders.

Hence, the values that underlie the company's strategy and the meaning employees find in working for the company are all important. This does not mean that substantive strategic and administrative issues should not be emphasized. But what separates a leader from a competent professional manager is the ability to build an organization that is a source of self-fulfillment and personal integrity for its members. This is not a new observation. Philip Selznick, a pioneer in the study of leadership, has described a leader as "primarily an expert in the promotion and protection of values." He describes a leader's task in this way:

> . . . to infuse [an organization] with value beyond the
> technical requirements of the task at hand. . . . Whenever
> individuals become attached to an organization or a way
> of doing things as persons rather than as technicians, the
> result is a prizing of the device for its own sake. From
> the standpoint of the committed person, the organization
> is changed from an expendable tool into a valued source
> of personal satisfaction. . . . It is the task of leadership,
> in embodying purpose, to fit the aims of the organization
> to the spontaneous interests of the groups within it, and
> conversely to bind parochial group egotism to larger loy-
> alties and aspirations.[2]

The main task of leadership is energizing followers to

take actions that support higher corporate purposes and not their own self-interests. Companies that rely solely on elaborate systems of transactions through which people exchange time and effort for money, security, and status, do not fulfill employees' deepest needs. These systems are based on what the philosopher Robert Nozick calls "capitalist acts between consenting adults."[3] If well managed, such exchanges can lead to sound—but not outstanding—performance; this is because they rely on arm's-length, unemotional, calculating relationships. They lack the focus, energy, commitment, and creativity that come from appeals to deeper values.

In his pathbreaking book *Leadership*, Pulitzer Prize winner James MacGregor Burns stresses the moral character of leadership. He distinguishes values-driven leadership—which he calls "transforming" and "transcending" leadership—from "transactional" leadership, in which leaders exchange money, power, status, and "perks" for the actions they want their followers to take. Burns writes:

> [Transforming] leadership occurs when one or more persons engage with others in such a way that leaders and followers raise one another to higher levels of motivation and morality. Their purposes, which might have started out as separate but related . . . become fused. Power bases are linked not as counterweights but as mutual support for common purpose. Transforming leadership ultimately becomes moral in that it raises the level of human conduct and ethical aspirations of both leader and led, and thus it has a transforming effect on both. . . . Transcending leadership is dynamic leadership in the sense that the leaders throw themselves into a relationship with followers, who will feel "elevated" by it and often become more active themselves, thereby creating new cadres of leaders.[4]

Organizations play an enormous role in meeting basic human needs and aspirations. These needs are not only financial security and material well-being; they include a desire to be creative and to work for some worthwhile purpose. Thus a leader has two basic responsibilities: to infuse a company with a purpose and values that others can identify with personally, and to create an environment in which people are encouraged to address problems and opportunities with creativity and deep personal commitment. In carrying out these responsibilities, leaders make manifest their own beliefs about human nature and organizations.

The Intrinsic Work Ethic

Before the Reformation, some philosophers believed that people were trapped by the necessity of working. Plato and Aristotle thought that a life of leisure and reflection, as embodied in the concept of the philosopher-king, was the only fit life. Toil was equated with slavery. In the Middle Ages, in accord with ancient Judeo-Christian belief, work was considered a wearisome and painful task that helped humans atone for their sinfulness.

The Reformation gave birth to the doctrine of the calling, the belief that God called everyone to a productive vocation in which they served the common good and increased God's glory. Wasting time was a sin. In *The Protestant Ethic and the Spirit of Capitalism*, Max Weber observed that the doctrine of the calling held special significance for the Puritans, the group that heavily influenced the early United States:

> For everyone without exception God's Providence has
> prepared a calling, which he should profess and in
> which he should labour. And this calling is not, as
> it was for the Lutheran, a fate to which he must submit and which he must make the best of, but God's
> commandment to the individual to work for the divine
> glory.[5]

In the United States, beginning in the late eighteenth century, the belief in a calling gradually became secularized. As the Industrial Revolution progressed, the concept of usefulness gradually replaced the concept of the calling. To produce and build was a social duty—a conviction that helped many to surmount the challenges of the American frontier.

Later, two other beliefs extended the notion of social duty. The first was the idea that people could improve their lots through diligent hard work. Second, work came to be seen as a creative act, one that enabled people to make a difference in the world. The sociologist Peter Berger has described the power of these beliefs:

> If work means to build a world, then it entails, in a religious perspective, a repetition or imitation of the divine acts by which the world was originally built—and perhaps even a competition with these divine acts, as the myth of Prometheus suggests. To work is no light matter. To work is to mime creation itself.[6]

These beliefs live on, albeit with difficulty. The specialization of industrialized work has reduced the opportunities for individual creativity, weakened the link between hard work and success, and distanced workers from the products of their efforts. As a result, as Karl Marx predicted a century ago, many workers are alienated. For Marx, man's alienation—from himself, from nature, and from other men—originated with the separation of the individual from the product of his work. The more of his life that he contributed to routine industrial work, the more he was demeaned. Marx held this view, in part, because he saw in a capitalistic society only two purposes for work: to earn wages needed to sustain life and to help capitalists accumulate capital. Marx wrote:

> The more the worker externalizes himself in his work, the more powerful becomes the alien, objective world that he creates opposite himself, the poorer he becomes himself in his inner life and the less he can call his own . . . . The life that he has lent to the object affronts him, hostile and alien.[7]

This battle between work as an alienating experience and work as a creative, fulfilling one continues today. Recognizing this, leaders strive to make their subordinates' work a source of satisfaction for deep inner needs, whether serving a worthwhile purpose or exercising creativity.

In a 1982 poll, Daniel Yankelovich asked people which of the following statements they most agreed with:

1. I have an inner need to do the very best job I can regardless of pay.
2. Work is a mere business transaction, I work only as much as I get paid.
3. Working for a living is one of life's necessities. I would not do it if I didn't have to.

Seventy-eight percent of the people identified with the first view, 7 percent identified with the second view, and 15 percent identified with the third. When asked how much control they felt they had over the effort they gave their jobs, 88 percent of those polled said they had a great deal of control. However, when asked whether they used this freedom to fulfill their "inner need to do the very best job," only 16 percent said that they did.[8]

Yankelovich's findings suggest that managers have failed to draw upon their employees' deep reserves of energy and commitment, particularly their need to do the very best job possible. Outstanding performance will come from the "hearts and minds" of employees attracted and motivated by higher values. The leader's job is to harness people's deep needs and aspirations.

Creativity and Meaning through Work

What are the needs that people seek to fulfill through their work? Beyond financial reward, status, security, and the prospect of career advancement, people value work that enables them to contribute to *worthwhile purposes*, that challenges their *creativity*, and that gives them a sense of *pride and accomplishment*. Belonging to a financially successful team is important but not enough. Work can be more than a means of gaining money, power, and prestige. As Eric Fromm has observed, the purely transactional view of work can lead to boredom, dissatisfaction, apathy, and alienation. The worker comes to "hate himself, because he sees his life passing by, without making any sense beyond the momentary intoxication of success."[9]

But this state is not inevitable. Working creatively for a worthwhile purpose can help people achieve their potentials and give their lives greater meaning. Eric Fromm writes:

> Work is not only an inescapable necessity for man. Work is also his liberator from nature, his creator as a social and independent being. . . . In the process of work he separates himself from nature, from the original unity with her, but at the same time unites himself with her again as her master and builder. The more his work develops, the more his individuality develops. In molding nature and re-creating her, he learns to make use of his powers, increasing his skill and his creativeness.[10]

If a company's purpose is defined in terms of the wider economic and social benefits of its products or services, people's contributions to fulfilling that purpose can bring increased meaning to their work. One executive expanded on this:

> Business does not exist merely to produce more goods and services, or better goods and services for more people, though that is no small part of its task. Business also, particularly in these days, affords the principal or the only means whereby individual men and women may gain the satisfaction of accomplishing something more than merely sustaining their own lives.[11]

In a small way, a person's contribution leaves a legacy and makes a claim on immortality.

The Company as Community

No one can single-handedly help others achieve meaning in work. Day by day, it is the organization as a whole that makes a difference. A company is much more than a political arena or one strong person's instrument for achieving economic ends. Companies are above all communities, in which people seek to meet a wide range of personal needs.

As communities, organizations shape the behavior of members not only through compensation systems, reporting relationships, and subunit interests, but also through norms, values, loyalties, aspirations, and unwritten rules. Shared values provide the basic assumptions that determine how people in a company perceive problems, seek alternative solutions, and make decisions. Thus values are critical to channeling behavior. Since they are grounded in basic beliefs about humanity and have a moral character, they tap fundamental human motivations. These motivations have much greater potential power to influence behavior than do systems and structures. Ultimately, values have a profound effect on the execution of the company's strategy.

A leader's behavior sets a company's moral tone and reinforces its purposes. Thus how a leader acts is crucial to ensuring that decisions promote and defend values. But, contrary to common belief, strong leadership is not a "one-man show." Constraints on time, energy, and expertise limit the impact a single person can make, as do decentralized management, diversified businesses, or geographically dispersed operations. In all but the smallest companies, the direct action of senior executives can only partially influence day-to-day behavior. For these reasons, the *company* itself should be the object of loyalty and commitment, the source of meaningful purpose, not the personality or behavior of a single outstanding person.

Although in practice employees' needs and values can take many forms, they have four basic factors in common. First, employees value adequate pay and acceptable levels of security, which companies must provide. Second, people want to take pride in their work. In particular, people value work that results in products and services that are outstanding in some way. They also value work that helps them develop their skills, that challenges them fully, that they accomplish through teamwork with others whom they like, respect, and trust, and that involves treating others fairly and honestly.

Third, people want to put their personal stamps on endeavors and develop their own potentials more fully. Fourth, people want their efforts to contribute to a worthwhile purpose, to know that their efforts make a difference.

Each of these assumptions about values relates to what an organization does, to the products or services a company provides, and to the behavior of its members. In Western countries, these values have roots in the Judeo-Christian culture, which sets ideals of honesty, fairness, individual freedom, and mutual responsibility in human relations, honors self-sacrifice for worthwhile ends, and stresses that the aims of life and work go beyond material reward and personal gratification.

THE PHILOSOPHY IN ACTION

Why do institutionalized values have a powerful effect on economic performance? The answer lies in several factors. When values and beliefs become embodied in work, they can intensify employees' commitment, enthusiasm, and drive, making a company a much stronger competitor. Shared values can give employees the incentive to work longer hours and do harder, more careful work. Shared values can also lower costs. To some degree, they replace financial compensation with psychic rewards, and they are also a form of compensation that can attract more highly skilled and experienced employees. When serving a worthwhile, creative purpose, employees can become intensely committed to satisfying customers' needs. Ultimately this is the bedrock of competitive advantage.

By generating deeper personal commitment and engaging more of the personalities and lives of people in their work, shared values may lead to much greater creativity and innovation. People who achieve major breakthroughs usually become totally immersed in what they are doing. This commitment carries them through opposition and failure. In the words of John Gardner, "The highest levels [of creativity] can be expected in those lines of endeavor that involve man's emotions, judgment, symbolizing powers, aesthetic perceptions, and spiritual impulses."[12]

Values have another powerful effect. If they are widely and genuinely held in an organization, values such as trust, fairness, and respect for the individual can greatly improve the quality and accuracy of communication, the integrity of the decision-making process, and management's ability to evaluate personnel and projects. People take more risks when they feel confident that they will be treated fairly should they fail.

But how do managers who believe in the strengths of values establish a meaningful corporate purpose and infuse a set of values into their organizations? A leader's commitment to the purpose and values of an organization must be evident in all that he or she does. A leader must be an exemplar to the organization, demanding the highest standards of integrity, and be doggedly consistent in word and deed in all matters affecting the company's values.

Setting and Communicating Company Goals

First and foremost, a company's strategy must be defined in terms that include and *transcend* economics. A company's goal must be both quantitative and qualitative. In formulating goals and strategy, a leader must concentrate on three questions: What are the company's fundamental purposes and objectives? What values will enhance its strategy and the skills upon which its success depends? How can the company reinforce these key values? No matter how homespun the philosophy may appear, identifying a broad, meaningful purpose for a company is at once a creative and philosophical act. It requires a breadth of vision to grasp the broader purposes a company can serve.

A Hierarchy of Goals. Just as people have many needs and goals, so do organizations. In most outstanding companies, financial objectives are viewed as a means of achieving higher, more fundamentally important, nonfinancial purposes. These purposes embody the company's basic values and define the distinctive contribution it seeks to make to its owners, its employees, its customers, the communities in which it does business, and its other constituents, even its nation.

A sense of purpose is the first and most fundamental component of a company's strategy. It strongly shapes the second component, the company's business concept: the statement of the products or services it will sell and the description of how it will secure a competitive advantage in its markets. As it is focused through the business concept, the company's purpose translates into the third component of strategy—the company's economic objectives: its targets for profit, growth, market share, and rates of return.

Great business organizations are not built solely by pursuing growth in earnings per share, return on equity, or market share. For typical employees, the complex reality of their daily responsibilities is far removed from the financial interests of shareholders. The most effective goals have a qualitative element that counterbalances their quantitative elements and that clearly defines how decisions should be made in situations where interests conflict.

Outstanding managers are aware of the potential threat that the automatic pursuit of short-term economic opportunities poses to institutionalized values. Sometimes, they must sacrifice short-term economic opportunities that are incompatible with a company's basic values or goals. Ideally, the broader values to which the company's goals appeal should reinforce the company's economic objectives; regardless, the broader values cannot be replaced by narrower economic ones.

The company's goals have to be accepted by employees within the company; they should also help the company meet competitive challenges. Potentially, these two objectives can conflict. If the company's common purpose embraces shared values, however, these conflicts are substantially reduced. Fundamental—and thus more powerful—shared values and purposes, such as creativity and a contribution to something worthwhile, dominate parochial self-interest. Localitis yields to the pursuit of a common purpose.

Several of the leaders we talked to underscored this vital idea. Walter Wriston stated his beliefs in the following way:

> A lot of leadership is being able to articulate your value system and where you are going in ways people understand. I spend a lot of time trying to hold out before people the concepts of excellence, honesty, and integrity.
>
> In the corporation, as in your life, you have to have some benchmarks by which to operate. Whether it is the Boy Scout motto or FASB Rule Number 9, you have to have some framework. A corporation is a collection of individuals. Without a framework, you don't know what you are doing. The only thing that draws our different cultures together is our common value system. For example, collegial management is a value. You have to have trust between people, and that's based on a common set of values and a common set of procedures.

A Statement of Purpose.   Some of America's most successful companies—IBM, Johnson & Johnson, Hewlett-Packard, and Procter & Gamble—have long had credos or statements of belief that define the essential purposes for which the organizations exist and guide decision making. More recently, companies like Borg-Warner and Security Pacific Corporation have devoted considerable management time and effort to clearly defining their beliefs and infusing them into their organization. In each of these companies, managers work hard to ensure that their credos are meaningful statements, and not just sets of superfluous platitudes.

For example, at Johnson & Johnson, the credo states:

> We believe our first responsibility is to the doctors, nurses, and patients, to mothers, and all others who use

our products and services. In meeting their needs, everything we do must be of high quality. We must constantly strive to reduce our costs in order to maintain reasonable prices. Customers' orders must be serviced promptly and accurately. Our suppliers and distributors must have an opportunity to make a fair profit.

We are responsible to our employees, the men and women who work with us throughout the world. Everyone must be considered as an individual. We must respect their dignity and recognize their merit. They must have a sense of security in their jobs. Compensation must be fair and adequate, and working conditions clean, orderly, and safe. Employees must feel free to make suggestions and complaints. There must be equal opportunity for employment, development, and advancement for those qualified. We must provide competent management, and their actions must be just and ethical.

We are responsible to the communities in which we live and work and to the world community as well. We must be good citizens—support good works and charities and bear our fair share of taxes. We must encourage civic improvements and better health and education. We must maintain in good order the property we are privileged to use, protecting the environment and natural resources.

Our final responsibility is to our stockholders. Business must make a sound profit. We must experiment with new ideas. Research must be carried on, innovative programs developed, and mistakes paid for. New equipment must be purchased, new facilities provided, and new products launched. Reserves must be created to provide for adverse times. When we operate according to these principles, the stockholders should realize a fair return.

A striking aspect of this statement is the order in which the responsibilities are listed: first customers, next employees, then communities, and finally shareholders. Shareholders are not only last, they are expected to receive a fair, not a maximum, return. Nevertheless, Johnson & Johnson has consistently provided high returns to its shareholders. James Burke, chairman of Johnson & Johnson, believes that this ordering of priorities was "part of General Johnson's genius. He knew that everybody was constantly thinking about the bottom line and wanted to force them to think about these other issues."

IBM provides another clear example of the importance and impact of values. IBM's managers have built one of the world's greatest economic institutions through respect for the dignity and rights of the individual, a commitment to excellence in all endeavors, and superior customer service. These beliefs define how IBM employees throughout the company should relate, not only to each other but also to customers, suppliers, and communities. Thomas Watson, Jr., the former chairman of IBM, emphasized the fundamental importance of these values:

> I firmly believe that any organization, in order to survive and achieve success, must have a sound set of beliefs on which it premises all its policies and actions.
>
> Next, I believe that the most important factor in corporate success is faithful adherence to those beliefs.
>
> And finally, I believe that if an organization is to meet the challenges of a changing world, it must be prepared to change everything about itself except those beliefs as it moves through corporate life.
>
> In other words, the basic philosophy, spirit, and drive of an organization have far more to do with its relative achievements than do technological or economic resources, organizational structure, innovation, and timing. All these things weigh heavily in success. But they are, I think, transcended by how strongly the people in the organization believe in its basic precepts and how faithfully they carry them out.[13]

Basic beliefs have also been important in defining

Hewlett-Packard's strategy. HP's "Statement of Corporate Objectives" consists of seven explicit objectives. Four of these are highly value laden:

Customers: To provide products and services of the greatest possible value to our customers, thereby gaining and holding their respect and loyalty.

Our People: To help HP people share in the company's success, which they make possible; to provide job security based on their performance; to recognize their individual achievements; and to help them gain a sense of satisfaction and accomplishment from their work.

Management: To foster initiative and creativity by allowing the individual great freedom of action in attaining well-defined objectives.

Citizenship: To honor our obligations to society by being an economic, intellectual, and social asset to each nation and each community in which we operate.

For Hewlett-Packard, profit is the means to other ends. The company's objectives state that profits should be "sufficient to finance our company growth and to provide the resources we need to achieve our other corporate objectives."

Defending a company's values requires constant vigilance. In the final analysis, promoting and defending values is a responsibility that leaders can share but should never delegate. For example, when David Packard returned to Hewlett-Packard after serving in the Defense Department, he learned that to finance the expansion of its infant, hand-held calculator business, the company was planning to take on a large amount of long-term debt for the first time in its history. In the past, Packard had opposed long-term debt, a policy that was based largely on the company's loyalty to its employees. In downturns, HP management wanted to be able to "invest" in employees through a no-layoff policy, rather than divert scarce funds to service debt. It believed that relying totally on internally generated funds provided a discipline that ensured efficiency and encouraged the "design and development of each and every product so that it is considered a good value by our customers, yet is priced to include an adequate profit."

Packard decided that the debt issue threatened the company's fundamental values and approach to business, and called it off. His decision was based on a personal commitment to the company's values, and not simply on financial analysis of its capital structure. After making this decision, he concentrated on building the company's internal efficiencies—particularly through conserving working capital, improving profit margins, and controlling costs—to generate the needed capital.

Jean Riboud, the former chief executive officer of Schlumberger, the oil field services giant, expressed a similar belief, "When you fly through turbulence, you fasten your seat belt. The only seat belt I know in business turbulence is to determine for oneself a few convictions, a few guidelines, and stick with them."[14] The following account by an observer of the company indicates the pivotal role of values in the management of the company:

> Riboud thinks of the company as an extension of personal values—humility, loyalty, preserving faith in an idea, serving people, being trusting, being open-minded to different cultures, being ambitious and competitive and yet mindful of tradition. The key in a corporation or a government, Riboud says, is "motivating people and forging a consensus. . . . We are no longer in a society where the head of a corporation can just give orders," he says. People need to believe in something larger than themselves. To be successful, he thinks, a corporation must learn from the Japanese that "we have the responsibility that religion used to have." A good company must not be just a slave to profits; it must strive to perform a service and to beat its competitors. But more, he feels, it must measure itself against a higher standard, seeking perfection.[15]

James Burke has an almost evangelical belief in his company's credo and its contribution to Johnson & Johnson's performance. For example, he says that Johnson & Johnson could not have responded as quickly and as successfully as it did to the Tylenol crisis, if many levels of management had not shared a belief in the credo. He explains the importance of the credo this way:

> I believe in the credo with a passion because I believe in the long run every institution in society has to serve all of its constituencies or it doesn't survive.
>
> What the credo says is that the first thing you have to do is be totally involved with the people who use your product and services. If you don't, it's a simple fact of life you will die, because someone else will be.
>
> The second thing it says is that the most important raw material you have is the employees. It is their creative energies that do it, after all. Everybody has money and the other things required for success. What's really required is the creative ability of people.
>
> The third thing that it says is if you ignore the communities that you deal with—whether they be the local communities where you have your plants or state or federal communities or just the community of man—your employees and your customers are going to get involved in that process. It is going to redound to your detriment.
>
> Finally, if you do all these things and remind yourself that you are here for the stockholder, you will serve him well.[16]

Burke has demonstrated vigilance in the defense of J&J's values in a variety of ways. In 1979, he became concerned that some managers were treating the credo with tokenism, a signal that they needed to recommit to the values underlying the statement. He described the actions he took to address this:

I called a meeting of some twenty key executives and challenged them. I said, "Here's the credo. If we're not going to live by it, let's tear it off the wall. If you want to change it, tell us how to change it. We either ought to commit to it or get rid of it."

The meeting was a turn-on, because we were challenging people's personal values. By the end of the session, the managers had gained a great deal of understanding about and enthusiasm for the beliefs in the credo. Subsequently, the company president and I have met with small groups of managers all over the world to challenge the credo.

Now, I don't really think you can impose convictions or beliefs on someone else. However, I do believe that if I really understand what makes the business work, I can prompt you to think through the facts and come to see just how pragmatic the philosophy is, when it comes to running a business successfully. . . . And I think that's what happened here.

Finally, . . . goals that are not forcefully communicated give the appearance, at the least, that management is not committed to them. Therefore, they are not a stimulus to focused effort and commitment on the part of others. Uncertain commitment can allow conflicting values to develop and possibly flourish. This can be a principal source of internal conflict and politicization, as the "hidden agenda" becomes filled with issues that represent the struggle between proponents of competing values and goals.[17]

Managing Formal Systems and Structures

Systems and structures are secondary to values, which in themselves are a powerful source of control that reduces the need for formal systems. Furthermore, the way systems and structures are managed can either reinforce or erode key values, consequently determining the degree to which employees fulfill a range of important personal needs.

Leaders continually need to ask whether changes in personnel, organizational structure, or systems will promote key values more effectively than do current arrangements. For example, a detailed, structured strategic planning and capital budgeting system installed to improve the quality of strategic decision making could at the same time discourage initiative, promote widespread second-guessing by staff and superiors, expand paperwork, and foster a bureaucratic mentality and "analysis paralysis." These systems often take decisions away from the managers who are most familiar with the products and markets.

At Lincoln Electric Company, the world's leading manufacturer of arc welding equipment, clearly articulated values that motivate each person result in harder work and increased creativity. As a result, the company has built a remarkable competitive record in an environment in which several major companies, including General Electric, were forced out of the business. It is one U.S. "rustbelt" manufacturing company that has prospered.

Founder James Lincoln translated belief in the individual; production of a worthwhile, low-cost, quality product that meets the customer's needs; and the "fair" distribution of the company's economic surplus among employees, customers, and shareholders, into a management system. He expressed his beliefs, which have become part of the social fabric of Lincoln Electric, in this way:

> Development in many directions is latent in every person. The difficulty has been that few recognize that fact. Fewer still will put themselves under the pressure or by chance are put under the pressure that will develop them greatly. . . .
>
> If the worker does not get a proper share [of the surplus], he does not desire to develop himself or his skill. The worker must have a reward that he feels is commensurate with his contribution. . . .
>
> There is no hard and fast rule to cover this division, other than the following. The worker (which in-

cludes management), the customer, the owner, and all
those involved must be satisfied that they are properly
recognized or they will not cooperate, and cooperation is
essential to any and all successful applications of incentives. . . .

        Most companies are run by hired managers,
under the control of stockholders. As a result, the goal of
the company has shifted from service to the customer to
making larger dividends for stockholders. The present
policy of operating industry for stockholders is unreason-
able. The rewards now given to him are far too much. He
gets income that should really go to the worker and the
management. The usual absentee stockholder contributed
nothing to efficiency. He buys a stock today and sells it
tomorrow. He often doesn't even know what the company makes. Why should he be rewarded by large dividends?[18]

        Its compensation system is an excellent example of
using systems to reinforce values and focus individual effort
on substance. Even though Lincoln makes complex ma-
chinery, a collective endeavor that makes it very difficult to
single out individual contributions, the company's reward
and measurement system relies on piecework wages and very
large merit bonuses based on corporate profits and the employee's dependability, output, ideas, and cooperation. The
bonuses often exceed the employee's regular annual pay; yet
these bonuses leave a residual that provides an attractive return on equity for shareholders. The system reinforces the
company's values by increasing the sense of ownership of
one's work and by increasing individual initiative. The result
has been large, consistent increases in productivity that have
been the bedrock of Lincoln's competitive advantage.

       Paving the Way to Autonomy. Many difficult deci-
sions involve value judgments. If employees share values,
their decisions are more likely to reflect the direction top management desires. People who share common values and purposes will feel less conflict between their personal interests

and those of their company. Consequently, managers need fewer systems and reporting structures to scrutinize and direct others.

Schlumberger exemplifies the way such values work. During the 1970s, when its industry was booming, the company could have been quite profitable with modest effort: Schlumberger had a near-monopoly position in wire-line logging, a critical technique for analyzing oil wells. Moreover, its most important employees were very difficult to supervise through conventional control and reporting systems. They were young engineers stationed for long periods alone or in very small teams in remote locations, such as deserts or jungles. Schlumberger relied on powerful values to overcome the problems of remoteness and complacency. The company committed itself to "perfection"—since high profits were after all ensured. It also cultivated in its employees the sense that they were members of an elite group of pioneers, engaged in "noble activity," proudly independent and achieving at the highest levels despite loneliness and arduous working conditions.

Johnson & Johnson has been able to reap the benefits of a highly autonomous organization without imposing stifling controls. James Burke discussed the importance of shared values to this ability:

> It is very hard to keep people pulling together if you have a real entrepreneurial environment. The very nature of the people that run our businesses—as well as the businesses themselves—is to go off on their own. "To hell with all that crap in New Brunswick [headquarters]. Who needs the Executive Committee? We know how to do it." People are also somewhat egocentric.
>
> How do we keep them all together? We try to do it by an overall set of principles and the fundamental moral precepts of the credo, which everyone buys into and responds to. At some level, everybody is a moral creature, whether they want to admit it or not.

At both Johnson & Johnson and Hewlett-Packard, corporate management uses autonomy to avoid bureaucracy, increase creativity and initiative, allow faster and better decisions, and generate a sense of commitment derived from a sense of ownership.

Resolving Conflicts

Conflict is a fact of life. Because of differing interests of the constituents a company serves and because of competition and disagreement among people and units inside a company, conflict is inevitable. Leaders must ask themselves these questions: Which individuals and subgroups are most strongly committed to the company's key values? How intense and how broad is the conflict between these and other groups? In answering them, a leader's overriding concern must be that the resolution of a conflict reinforce the company's critical values. This usually means that the "winners" should be people and units who share these values. If politically powerful members of a company don't share these values, they will soon erode. Fortunately, shared values can help reduce political maneuvering, thus reducing and often resolving conflict.

A leader must be able to identify conflicts that involve vital values and norms. This is possible only if a leader has a strong personal commitment to them. Because of this commitment, a leader cannot compromise on issues involving the company's basic values—regardless of the conflict that may ensue. The inconsistency and vacillation that inevitably result from negotiation and compromise greatly bar a leader's ability to get others to take a company's values seriously.

Managing Day by Day

Because they seek opportunities to build and defend values, leaders develop a wide range of informal relations with others. They use these personal dealings with others not simply to build consensus incrementally or to exercise direct control, but to show their commitment to their company's values. In implementing decisions, they ask themselves,

"How can I reinforce basic values through what I say and do and through the agenda I set in working with others? How can I explain my decisions and actions in terms of values that are basic to my company?"

Leaders who have values uppermost in their minds are unwilling to compromise or tolerate ambivalence about basic values. They need not have charismatic personalities or use memorable devices to dramatize their purposes. Instead they use their own examples and commitment to reinforce their purposes.

Informal personal contacts are opportunities to remind others of the broad mission of a company, to instill values, and to evaluate the degree to which key values are, in fact, influential in others' thinking and decisions. Informal contacts also create opportunities to test others' commitment to an organization's values through questions that touch on values as well as economics. Thus meetings should be open forums, not orchestrated affairs designed to reach predetermined outcomes.

A leader's pattern of action on issues—both big and small—will determine the extent to which others believe that a company truly stands for key values and that their leader personifies these values. When subordinates see a leader's conviction reflected in things that they value, this enhances their respect and admiration for him or her. Leaders should go to great lengths to avoid appearing inconsistent or acting in ways that communicate insincerity, the death knell of institutionalized values.

Encouraging Others' Commitment to Values. Other members of a top management team must share a leader's commitment and beliefs. Consequently, enormous attention must be paid to recruiting, hiring, training, and promoting. Rather than seeing strong subordinates as a threat, outstanding leaders see them as a necessity. James F. Lincoln, the founder of Lincoln Electric Company, observed, "A strong leader knows that if he develops his associates, he will be even stronger."

Because a company's culture can change the attitudes

and behavior of adults to only a limited degree, especially over short periods of time, a company must attract employees who already share somewhat its key values and whose needs are likely to be met by working there. Hiring or promoting solely on technical competence—without regard to values, needs, and loyalties—can be perilous.

Promotions should also reflect the strength of employees' commitment to the company's values, as well as their technical competence. By the same token, training should both clarify a company's values and provide technical skills. Only when a company is truly a meritocracy, in which values and technical competence are both recognized, does a sense of fairness and mutual trust fully develop. Trust, the linchpin of effective management, is predicated on this fair treatment and shared sense of values.

In dealing with people, leaders often face conflicts between driving others to achieve excellence and fostering values of openness, candor, trust, cooperation, and mutual respect among members of the organization. While being sensitive to issues of timing, they must convey a sense of urgency. This is particularly important in companies with high degrees of autonomy and in companies that value creativity and individual initiative. Excessive top-down intervention can undermine these values, but autonomy without high standards and accountability can result in lackadaisical performance.

Richard Munro considered coping with these tensions to be one of the most important aspects of his job. He explained:

> We run on a consensus basis. We have home-grown talent that has had a wide variety of experiences. We know each others' strengths, weaknesses, and idiosyncrasies. We have enormous respect for each other and are very decent to each other. Yet sometimes I think we are lulled by this respect. We pull our punches at times and have paid a price for it.
>
> I spend an enormous amount of time promoting

openness. I speak about it every chance I get. One of the most important things I do is protect this environment, which is quite fragile.

We don't believe in punishing people. We're an entrepreneurial company. We try like hell to encourage entrepreneurship in every way we can. We try and make sure people are not afraid to fail. If you have an environment in which people keep looking over their shoulders thinking, "If I stub my toe, there goes my career," it has an immense implication for how people address their day-to-day jobs, much less for things that are really innovative. When we make a mistake, we don't reach out and lash people. If you start flogging people the minute things go wrong, you are in deep trouble. You begin to shake the very nature of this company. Failure, especially highly visible failure, is very hard on a whole organization.

Finally, critical decisions—major financial commitments or changes in strategy, or "nonstrategic" matters, such as a vacancy in an important job or the manner in which an employee is disciplined—become key points of focus. These decisions are often disguised or embedded in issues that seem on the surface to be more benign. The leader must be able to detect these situations and understand what values other people in the organization perceive to be at stake.

Empathy is essential in identifying, promoting, and defending values that employees will cherish, that will stimulate exceptional efforts, and that will create competitive advantages. The greater this understanding, the more likely a leader's actions will reflect the values to which others dedicate themselves and for which they sacrifice. A leader must transform his or her genuine appreciation of others' values into goals and consistent actions that reinforce the shared values. Only actions based on shared values are seen as genuine.

But while a leader's profile may become less distinct, his or her actions have a continuing central significance, often becoming revered as symbols of the institutionalized values. The result can be the development of a folklore associated with the leader that helps define and defend the values. Hewlett-Packard has its "Bill and Dave" stories and Cray Research Inc. has its "Seymour" (Cray) stories that play a vital role in defining what these companies are. One widely accepted "Seymour" story holds that Seymour Cray, a sailing enthusiast, designs and builds a new sailboat each spring. After sailing it for the summer, he burns it to prevent next year's design from being confined by this year's. The symbolic value for state-of-the-art computer design is clear. When asked if the numerous Seymour stories are true, John Rollwagen, Cray's CEO replies, "If they weren't, I'd never tell anybody."[19]

When a values-driven leader's actions are successful in institutionalizing values in a company, the organization becomes the focus of loyalty instead of the leader. While subordinates have a sense that their accomplishments are their own, the leader's role in guiding the company becomes less distinct to the observer. As Lao-tsu, the ancient Chinese philosopher, said: "To lead the people, walk behind them. For the best leaders, people do not notice their existence. When the best leader's work is done, the people say, 'We did it ourselves!'"

NOTES

1. David E. Lilienthal, *Management: A Humanist Art* (New York: Columbia University Press, 1967), p. 18.
2. Philip Selznick, *Leadership in Administration* (New York: Harper & Row, 1957), pp. 17, 93–94.
3. Robert Nozick, *Anarchy, State, and Utopia* (New York: Basic Books, 1974), p. 163.
4. James MacGregor Burns, *Leadership* (New York: Harper & Row, 1978), pp. 4, 20.
5. Max Weber, *The Protestant Ethic and the Spirit of Capitalism*, trans. Talcott Parsons (New York: Charles Scribner's Sons, 1930), p. 160.
6. Peter L. Berger, "Some General Observations on the Problem of Work." In *The Human Shape of Work*, ed. Peter L. Berger (New York: Macmillan 1964), p. 212.

7. Karl Marx, *Selected Writings*, ed. David McLellan (Oxford: Oxford University Press, 1977), pp. 78–79.
8. Daniel Yankelovich, "The Work Ethic is Underemployed," *Psychology Today*, May 1982, p. 6.
9. Eric Fromm, *The Sane Society* (New York: Fawcett World Library, 1955), p. 164.
10. Ibid., p. 159.
11. Abram T. Collier, "Business Leadership and a Creative Society," *Harvard Business Review*, January–February 1968, p. 155.
12. John W. Gardner, *Self-Renewal* (New York: Harper & Row, 1971), p. 41.
13. Thomas Watson, Jr., "A Business and Its Beliefs," McKinsey Foundation Lecture (New York: McGraw-Hill, 1963), pp. 5–6.
14. Ken Auletta, *The Art of Corporate Success* (New York: Penguin, 1983), p. 98.
15. Ibid., pp. 123–124.
16. Presentation by James E. Burke at Harvard Business School, December 1983.
17. Ibid.
18. Norman Berg and Norman Fast, "The Lincoln Electric Company," 376-028. Boston: Harvard Business School, 1975.
19. Presentation by John Rollwagen at Harvard Business School, November 1984.

PART II

INTEGRITY AND THE DILEMMAS OF LEADERSHIP

INTRODUCTION

Each of the three views of leadership described in Part I—the political, directive, and values-driven—aspires to be a complete philosophy of management. Each proceeds from basic assumptions about human nature and organizations to form clear recommendations for day-to-day behavior. Each philosophy also reflects important traditions of thought about the nature of leadership, whether in religious, military, or government organizations, as well as more recent ideas about leadership in business organizations. Furthermore, each of the philosophies is credible. Managers can find their own assumptions and predispositions, and those of other managers, reflected in the three views.

But at this point, the philosophies diverge. Each starts with different views of human nature and these lead to very different patterns of action. Political leadership holds that man is motivated by self-interest and by a search for power, wealth, and coherence in the face of self-interested behavior by others. While not rejecting these realities, directive leadership argues that they are too limited for explaining people's motivation. Directive leadership believes that man is also a competitive creature driven to achieve. People want to take personal responsibility for their decisions and have the satisfaction of knowing they have won through their own efforts. Man has a strong, innate drive to realize his own potential or, in psychological terms, to self-actualize. As Maslow has said, "What man can be, he must be." As they strive for higher levels of attainment, people meld self-interest with corporate interest.

The values-driven leader takes the directive leader's view one step further and believes that people need to find meaning in life through their work. Meaning is derived from creativity in the service of worthwhile purposes. Creating something of value is the ultimate expression of one's individuality. Values-driven leadership holds that energy, commitment, and creativity are unleashed when a company harnesses these motives.

While a political leader sees people as fundamentally isolated and oriented toward their own needs, the directive and values-driven leaders see people as more dependent on and influenced by broader interests than their own. Thus it is a fundamental responsibility of leadership to help people realize their capabilities, lest these remain latent.

Because of these different beliefs, each philosophy strongly advocates a different answer to a critical question: What distinguishes managers who lead their companies to extraordinary performance from ordinary professional managers? This chapter and the five that follow it discuss five classic dilemmas of management and show how leaders following each of the three philosophies would attack them. They also provide practical guidance—in the form of prejudices—for resolving these dilemmas and reconciling the conflicts among the philosophies.

Undergirding our entire argument is a single, powerful, but complex idea that is encapsulated in the seemingly familiar notion of integrity. Everyone thinks they know what integrity is, and in a broad sense they are probably right. But the familiarity of the notion can mislead. The concept of integrity is a nexus of ideas and guidelines that is central to business leadership. Integrity and what it implies for resolving the conflicts among the three philosophies and the dilemmas of management are the subject of the rest of this book.

To a crippling degree, looking at the world through the lenses of the three philosophies simplifies reality. Each philosophy is, in effect, an intense spotlight that illuminates some of a leader's concerns, while leaving other important elements in shadow. While accurate, each offers only a partial view. Companies are not simply political arenas. Nor are they merely technical, economic instruments. Nor are they solely communities sharing norms and values.

Considering the philosophies jointly does not make them any less disquieting. Taken together, they raise more questions than they answer. Among these are three sets of important questions:

1. Do the patterns of action of individual managers tend to fall into one or another of the three categories suggested by the three philosophies? Do managers really base their actions on broad philosophies?
2. Which of the philosophies provides the best guidance for managers who want to lead their businesses to outstanding performance?
3. Are managers more likely to excel if they simply adapt their behavior to the demands of a particular situation, rather than follow one or another philosophy?

Some of these questions are much easier to answer than others. The first set, for example, asks whether the three philosophies describe alternative ways in which real managers approach their work. In broad terms, the answer to this question is yes. We believe that in certain respects, outstanding managers are closet philosophers. Few, of course, have encompassing, detailed philosophies of management that give them precise prescriptions for their daily work, but the leaders we have studied have been thoughtful and reflective. They have had definite predispositions and convictions. Moreover, the executives we interviewed had all reflected on their own approaches to leadership. They readily and clearly contrasted themselves with other senior executives who thought and behaved differently, and they confidently explained and justified their approaches to problems. They sought, and believed they had achieved, a consistency of behavior that reflected their own personal convictions about people and organizations. In short, the three philosophies are not a scheme for neatly pigeonholing managers, but they do capture fundamental predispositions. Outstanding leaders do not act, day by day, on the basis of precise rules derived from explicit philosophies, but they do believe that their actions are guided by coherent sets of convictions that they have drawn from their own beliefs and experiences.

Of the questions listed above, the last two are the most important. They move beyond mere description. They are questions of action. As such, their answers have powerful implications for the daily work of managers. In this introduction and the following six chapters, we respond to each of these questions. Because these questions are much more difficult to answer—they cannot be handled in a few sentences or paragraphs—the remainder of this book is essentially an answer to both of them.

INTEGRITY

To merely describe how conflicts among philosophies of leadership lead to management dilemmas is an academic exercise. Left hanging are critical, practical questions: How should a manager approach a specific situation involving one or more of the dilemmas? Do one or another of the three philosophies offer better practical guidance to managers? Or, is it better to ignore the broad philosophies and do what seems best in a particular situation?

Although simple answers are often advocated, none suffices. Taken one by one, each of the philosophies is too simple an approach for the wide diversity of situations that managers face. None can unambiguously resolve the dilemmas that managers routinely encounter.

Rather, guidance lies in a complex idea, that of integrity. Integrity may seem to some a familiar, Boy Scout trait whose main purpose is to ornament commencement addresses and other inspirational, but somewhat impractical ways of writing and speaking. But this is wrong.

Integrity lies at the very heart of understanding what leadership is. The word "integrity" suggests wholeness and coherence. It also suggests rightness, a sense of moral soundness. But of what? Just what are the elements that cohere and display integrity? The answer to these questions emerged from the interviews we conducted, but did so almost accidentally.

We did not ask the seven leaders we interviewed about integrity, nor did we set out to learn about it. Nevertheless, we heard, again and again, a clear, common vision of how these leaders aspired to run their companies and the kinds of organizations they were trying to build. Even though these executives were practical men of affairs who have run large, complex businesses, and even though they had competed intensely to reach the top positions in their companies, their descriptions of what they hoped to accomplish and how they wanted to lead mingled visionary aspirations with tough-minded realism. What they aspired to was a consistency and coherence among what they believed, how they managed, and the kinds of organizations they wanted to build. It is precisely this consistency—of personal beliefs and values, daily working behavior, and organizational aims—that we call integrity.

Integrity is the rationale for the prejudices described in the rest of this book, prejudices that can guide managers when they face dilemmas raised by the conflicts among the three philosophies of leadership. Moreover, understanding integrity in leadership helps to answer the two vital practical questions posed earlier in this chapter: Is one of the philosophies of leadership "truer" or more useful than the others? Are managers more likely to succeed if they simply concentrate on the demands of the situation rather than follow some broader guidelines? Because integrity is pivotal, the next several pages explain in detail each of its basic elements: personal beliefs and values, organizational aims, and individual behavior.

Personal Values

In our interviews, there was a strong, common pattern of responses to the question: What personal values are more likely to lead to outstanding managerial performance? This pattern emerged when we asked the CEOs what advice they would give to a group of outstanding middle managers who aspired to become heads of companies. It also emerged when we asked them what personal traits had helped them (and the other members of their top management teams) lead their companies to outstanding performance. Among the answers, three dominated.

Strong Personal Ethics. The first was having a strong set of personal ethical standards—principally honesty and fairness. Again and again, executives told us that these characteristics are the fundamental source of trust and loyalty in an organization. They believed that the widely accepted conflict between high ethical values and economic performance was, in the long term, a false dichotomy. Such ethical values lie at the heart of the organizations these leaders had spent much of their careers trying to create. (James Burke had Johnson & Johnson prepare a study showing a correlation between companies with "credos" expressing high ethical standards and significantly above-average, long-term returns to shareholders.)

Ralph Bailey commented, "I am repeatedly struck by how many outstanding corporate leaders have strong religious beliefs." He did not intend to argue that religious convictions by themselves were necessary or sufficient for outstanding business leadership. But his observation places the first set of personal characteristics—high ethical standards—in an important light. Outstanding leaders have sources of inner direction. The beliefs need not be religious. But they do provide a compass, set by important life experiences, that guides leaders through the daily pushes and pulls of managerial work.

Positive Belief in Others. The second personal value was a strong belief in the goodwill and latent ability of other people. The leaders we interviewed believed that the high-caliber people they had attracted to their organizations could be motivated to act for reasons beyond personal, economic self-interests. This faith was not simple näiveté. As a general proposition, most people, most of the time, may be captives of their own self-interests. But organizations select and develop their personnel, and reward certain kinds of behavior while discouraging others. Top executives also set examples of the behavior that they want to see followed. In short, an organization—and especially its top executive ranks—is a special and select environment. Leaders can determine who joins this environment and can, in important ways, shape the behavior of people in it. Of course, self-interest persists. But the leaders we interviewed believed that it could be shaped, tempered, and sometimes subordinated to broader objectives. This belief was reflected in their willingness to delegate responsibility, reduce bureaucratic oversight, and listen. They understood how much they could learn from subordinates by listening to them.

Compelling Vision. The third shared value was a strong, compelling vision for their companies. This vision, which had its source in a personal and imaginative creativity that extended beyond analysis, was embodied in actions that reflected initiative, risk taking, and an unswerving commitment to its achievement. This was a vision not only of how the company was to achieve a competitive advantage, but also of the kind of organization the company was to be and how this was to be accomplished. Values coupled with a competitive vision provided a powerful compass that enabled these leaders to keep their companies on strategic course, to differentiate important issues from unimportant ones, and to evaluate more readily potential second-order consequences—the ripple effects—of their actions. Much like superb athletes—whose training allows them to react on instinct, not on reasoned judgment—leaders with strong values and a clear vision of their companies' futures can respond intuitively as well as analytically to the complex, rapidly changing conditions in their companies.

Organizational Aims

The second, central element of integrity for the executives we interviewed was an idealistic, almost visionary description of the aims they had for their organizations. We refer to these aims as the "ideal company."

The many characteristics of the ideal company cluster in five groups. The first is an overriding concern that the company be a *meritocracy* of high-caliber talent. Recruiting, developing, and promoting people with first-rate interpersonal skills and intellectual ability is an absolute prerequisite for outstanding results. These are the wellsprings of a company's creativity and ability to innovate. Alexander d'Arbeloff asserted:

> Without talent, I don't care what you do, it is hopeless. You have to have a system that identifies, attracts, and develops talent. All of the people I've known who have built companies are absolute fanatics on finding talent. But the problem goes beyond technical competence. It is the attitude, the desire to excel, and the fit with our culture.

Making a company a meritocracy attracts and helps to keep talent. Walter Wriston stressed that the first thing his company stood for was that "people can go as far as their talents will take them without regard to age, race, sex, or whatever."

The second characteristic of the ideal company is that *people have a deeply shared sense of the company's goals and purpose.* This means a clear understanding of the organization's economic goals, the strategic logic underlying them, and individual roles in contributing to these goals. It also means that the corporate purpose stimulates commitment and effort. The importance of shared purpose was reflected in the frequency with which these executives referred to their companies with metaphors that involved community, family, or athletic teams. Walter Wriston observed, "One reason for our success is that we have created a spirit of family." He stressed the importance of getting people to

> live in each other's pockets by practicing living together in all kinds of circumstances. Managing a great corporation is like a football team. The tight end turns his head and the ball is sitting there. It's not there because the

quarterback is all that smart, but because they have been practicing that together for a long time.

At Johnson & Johnson, divisions were referred to as a "family of companies." A sense of community not only increases cohesiveness and the likelihood people will share a vision, but also fosters an environment that accepts the challenge of high standards in pursuit of that vision.

The third characteristic these executives sought was *open and candid communication, even to the point of heated, emotional debate.* Employees were expected to communicate in this way with their peers and subordinates as well as with their bosses. Open communication was recognized as a two-way street. It helped to ensure that information flowed to where it was needed—up, down, and across the organization. It also ensured that people tested plans and proposals through vigorous debate, and that information was less tainted by political concerns. We often heard comments such as "the door is always open" (one CEO's office had no door). Richard Munro claimed, "Openness is something a guy in my job literally never stops thinking about." Ralph Bailey explained:

> The only way to get at the truth is to really go at each other—and we have vigorous arguments. The objective is to make damn sure that everything has been heard. In one instance, one voice turned the whole executive committee around and saved us from a $500 million loss.

One CEO told us about a major competitor whose performance was eroding under marketplace pressures. The competitor gathered its major executives at a retreat in New Hampshire and installed an "electronic gizmo" that allowed them to vote anonymously on issues raised in discussion. When he heard about this, the CEO told his policy committee, "Can you imagine a group of senior people who can't talk to each other!?" He later reflected, "In our store, it is so different. Our people just say, 'You are just full of Christmas turkey this morning'—and that's it."

The executives we interviewed recognized that candid information meant people had to understand they would
not be punished for conveying bad news or for failing in a
well-reasoned, risk-taking effort. Quite the contrary. In their
companies, discipline was reserved for those who failed to be
candid; rewards sometimes went to those who made diligent
efforts but failed.

The fourth aim is to *create an environment in which
subordinates have substantial autonomy.* We heard three reasons for this objective. The leaders we interviewed wanted
subordinates to have a sense of ownership that increased their
commitment to the company and the effort they expended.
They believed the closer to the customer a decision is made,
the faster and better it is likely to be. They wanted to combat
bureaucratic tendencies by minimizing the decision steps, organizational layers, and number of people involved in each
decision.

Finally, the executives stressed a fifth characteristic,
usually with strong conviction: *a desire that high ethical standards pervade the company.* The most commonly mentioned
values were honesty, fairness, mutual respect and trust, and
compassion and sensitivity in the exercise of power. These
forceful men emphasized the responsibilities that accompany
power. Ralph Bailey observed, "You must make it known
within the organization, and demonstrate it by your personal
actions, that power must be exercised very carefully and with
a great deal of humility and compassion." Walter Wriston
added, "People have to know at the end of the day, after much
frustration and false starts, that they will get an honest and
compassionate answer about human beings—that people will
get an honest break. Compassion is part of honesty in dealing
with people. We try to weed out those without compassion."

The five characteristics of this ideal company form a
cohesive whole. They reinforce and strengthen each other to
such an extent that eliminating any one of them endangers the
others. For example, a clear shared purpose provides a sense
of direction and sets standards of achievement. Without high-

caliber talent, a company will lack the intellectual capacity to come up with creative solutions to problems, and it will lack the skills to translate these solutions into practice. Moreover, without strong people, a company cannot achieve the high standards of performance that lead to outstanding results. Open communication ensures that the company's purpose will be widely shared. Furthermore, the company's decisions will reflect the best thinking of the members of the company because information will flow freely to those who need it and because critical issues will have been discussed openly and critically. Autonomy, one of the prerequisites for attracting talented people, means that decisions can be made more quickly, nearer the customer and the source of operating information, and can be made with fewer bureaucratic controls. A clear, shared purpose and open communication reduce the risk that decisions made autonomously will not serve a company's long-term objectives.

For two reasons, ethical standards stand at the center of these characteristics. The first is that ethical standards are prerequisites for achieving the four other characteristics. For example, the execution of a company's strategy will involve hard decisions in which some managers' views will prevail. Some will win, some will lose. If all parties believe that these decisions have been made fairly through open debate by people whom they respect and trust, they will pull together more effectively to implement whatever decisions have been made. Furthermore, respect for and trust in the decision makers will encourage people to be candid and share information, rather than massage and package information for political ends.

Trust combined with clear, shared expectations also promotes the belief that people will be fairly evaluated. When people have confidence that their performances will be judged fairly—even if they should fail when taking well-reasoned, well-executed risks—they are more likely to take the initiative to champion and implement creative ideas.

Autonomy is fundamentally a matter of trust and mutual respect. It rests on the belief that without direct oversight someone else will make important decisions in desired ways. It presupposes that those given autonomy will be honest, candid, and open—especially about surprises and bad news—so corrective action can be taken quickly. To some degree, elaborate systems to oversee managers are a measure of lack of trust in subordinates' abilities and motivations. Finally, highly talented and ambitious people can easily collide with each other—a prospect that is reduced when they trust and respect each other.

The second, very important reason ethical standards form the core of the ideal organization is that these ethical standards are personal. They reflect the attitudes, judgments, experiences, and values of men and women responsible for leading companies. Ethical standards are the crucial link between leaders' aims for their organizations, on the one hand, and their own personal beliefs and actions, on the other. And integrity, as noted above, is fundamentally a matter of coherence and consistency among organizational aims, personal values and beliefs, and individual behavior.

For Jean Riboud, the late chairman of Schlumberger, the oil field services company, these convictions were forged during the two years he spent at Buchenwald and later working with Marcel Schlumberger, his mentor. Riboud learned to think for himself. He learned to sort out his subordinates— sometimes almost ruthlessly—based on their own ability to be forceful, independent thinkers; he learned to judge others on their character. And he became intensely committed to high, almost perfectionistic standards.[1] As for Riboud, the companies to which outstanding leaders commit their effort, intelligence, and attention are expressions of themselves. Because they closely identify with their organizations, these leaders seek to make their companies expressions of the beliefs and values they hold important.

The leaders we interviewed were realistic about their efforts to create an ideal organization—they were striving to reach a Camelot, but knew they never would. They acknowledged that their companies were far from this ideal. To the extent that they had built organizations based on trust and loyalty, they were aware these foundations were fragile and could easily be destroyed. But this did not deter them from aiming for these ideals.

Values in Action

A leader's actions are the pivotal link between personal beliefs and organizational aims. But the problem of achieving integrity through action is that much of the critical work of senior managers involves resolving basic *dilemmas* whose origins lie in the different assumptions and recommendations of the three philosophies. Each of the philosophies suggests different ways of thinking about problems and different ways of taking action.

Consider, for example, the following situation. An executive in charge of the French subsidiary of a large U.S. multinational concluded that his company needed to change its strategy and operations dramatically. Despite his company's success in customizing its products and operating through decentralized plants, with a separate sales force and customized products for each nation in Europe, he believed the company could gain significant competitive advantages by reducing costs through a Europeanwide strategy of product-line standardization and mass production. The new strategy would involve consolidating plants and shifting the attitudes and practices of the sales force. The company's sales force would have to sell more on the basis of price than on prestige and long-term customer relationships.

In this situation, the executive faced several classic dilemmas. Two of the three philosophies of leadership, the political view and the directive view, pulled him in very different directions. For example, he had to decide whether to pursue a general, flexible, opportunistic approach to implementing his strategy or to take a clear, precise, much more direct approach that would translate his vision into sharp statements of goals, clear organizational responsibilities, and precise standards for accountability and follow-through. He chose the former. Because he did not want to mobilize resistance, he did not announce a long-term plan to rationalize, consolidate, and replace the current successful strategy. Instead, he started by altering a minor part of the product line, a part that did not threaten the core manufacturing and sales operations. Later, he seized an opportunity to start a price war which ultimately left the company little choice but to proceed all the way with standardization. In effect, he took the political path.

He also knew that his strategy would clash with his division's familiar, well-established ways of doing business. Facing the dilemma of confrontation versus compromise, he chose to compromise. He did not try to force his will on the organization, but rather let the preferences of the country managers strongly influence what he did. For example, even though he knew his Europeanwide product line would eventually make the current national product lines obsolete, he let the country managers make further investments in their own national lines and manufacturing operations. Finally, he faced the conflict between long-term, more intangible considerations and short-term pressing ones. The short-term factors were the desires of each of the national baronies in Europe to keep running their businesses in the ways they had in the past. Because of the resistance he knew he would immediately face should he proceed quickly and directly, he was willing to delay the achievement of his long-term plan and to alter its implementation.

None of these decisions was easy to make but, guided strongly by the political philosophy of leadership, this executive's approach ultimately succeeded. Progress was slow, however. It took over twelve years to fully implement the strategy. Moreover, because he kept his strategy vague, corporate headquarters in the United States had expectations for performance that were inconsistent with the strategy and almost abandoned the strategy—and the executive—halfway through its implementation. The dilemmas and decisions he

faced were extremely difficult and the assumptions and guidelines of two of the philosophies of leadership pulled him
strongly in opposite directions.

Integrity and the Dilemmas of Management

Our argument about integrity and leadership is not
simple. The reason is that the subject itself is complicated and
involves many subtle considerations. But the broad skeleton
of our view may be summarized briefly.

The work of management is, in large measure, the
resolution of vexing dilemmas. Three persuasive philosophies
of leadership provide very different guidelines for managers
who face these dilemmas. And the philosophies raise questions. Which philosophy should a manager follow? Is one
more likely than another to lead to outstanding performance?
Or, should the whole notion of philosophies and guidelines be
cast aside in favor of resolving each situation on the basis of its
peculiar demands?

The answers to these questions lie in understanding
the role of integrity in leadership. Integrity is a consistency
and coherence among three elements. One is a leader's aspirations for his or her organization. Another is a leader's own
personal values. While these are conceptually separable, they
are in reality intricately intertwined. The men and women
who helped to build outstanding business organizations commit much of their adult lives and almost all of their intelligence and effort to this task. The organizations they build are
expressions of themselves and their values. Because they
identify closely with their organizations and have committed
so much of their lives to them, these companies reflect the
beliefs and values that they hold most important.

Left alone, however, organizational aims and personal aspirations run the risk of being irrelevant. They must be
translated into action through behavior that will move a company toward the ideal organization, one that is consistent with
the leader's personal values in a dilemma-dominated world.

That is, the broad notion of integrity must be translated into practical guidance that steers its way between tidy, cookie cutter, "how to do it" lists and the fundamentally vacuous advice that "it all depends." This guidance takes the form of prejudices. The prejudices described in the remainder of this book are ways of translating personal values and organizational aims into actions and decisions that resolve the recurring dilemmas of managerial life and lead to outstanding company performance and individual leadership.

NOTE

1. Ken Auletta. *The Art of Corporate Success* (New York: Penguin, 1983).

Chapter 4

CLARITY AND PRECISION VERSUS
FLEXIBILITY

Whether or not they are aware of it, managers confront the first dilemma—the tension between general, flexible approaches to problems and specific, precise, clear approaches—in myriad ways. The dilemma arises when they set goals and choose ways to communicate them, evaluate plans and results, create management systems, and respond to the countless tactical and strategic issues they encounter every day.

Consider the following situations:

Under competitive pressure from the Far East, you must cut your company's prices and, thus, its manufacturing costs. You have concluded that the best way to do this would be to standardize and rationalize your manufacturing process. You have developed a fairly specific plan that entails consolidating plants and significantly reducing employment over the next few years. It would also reduce the responsibilities of some of the remaining managers. You are concerned that a clear statement of your plans could not only have an adverse impact on morale and mobilize resistance, but it could also cause some talented people to leave the company. On the other hand, you need the cooperation and input of many people to carry out the new strategy. How clearly and specifically would you communicate the new strategy?

A newly appointed manager, who reports to you, meets you in the hall. He asks how you think he should handle a problem with a major customer. You recognize that this is a difficult and important problem, and one you have experience with, but the problem is his direct responsibility, not yours. Do you give him a specific answer to his question? Or do you say, "That's a tough one. Let me know what you decide?" Would you, either directly or through probing questions, direct him to the solution that you think is most appropriate? Or would you do something else?

An experienced plant manager presents you with a funding request for a piece of new equipment. You find his presentation vague. You probe further, but his responses say, in essence, "Trust me—I've thought this through." Do you ask him to go back and analyze his proposal further, possibly giving him specific guidance as to what areas to examine? Would you state precisely what your expectations are for the equipment and tell him, "I'm really not on board with your thinking. Keep me posted"? Do you let him know that you are displeased with the seeming lack of depth of his analysis and preparation? Or would you take another approach?

Underlying all three situations is the tension between being specific and direct on the one hand, and being general, somewhat vague, and indirect on the other hand. The stakes are high. At issue are the clarity of purpose and direction, the caliber of specific decisions, a leader's future flexibility to change course, the sense of ownership subordinates feel toward their responsibilities, the potential for resentment and resistance by subordinates, and the values important to an organization. Given the magnitude of the stakes, what predisposition, if any, should a leader have in deciding what action to take? Each of the three philosophies of leadership provides a different answer.

Consider the first situation. The political philosophy suggests the manager should handle the situation flexibly and be careful, perhaps a little vague, about the threatening aspects of the strategy. This approach could reduce the resistance from people whose interests would be harmed by standardized manufacturing. The manager would also have more flexibility to maneuver as circumstances change. To lead the organization, a manager should react skillfully to ideas, opportunities, and problems originating with subordinates— moving forward on those that further the strategy, reshaping some to make them consistent with the strategy, and putting others on the back burner. By reacting to others' ideas rather than promoting his own, the leader gives his subordinates a greater sense that they own the resulting strategy.

On the other hand, the directive philosophy holds that to rationalize manufacturing successfully the manager should be specific and clear about goals. A manager's overriding issue should be to establish the right strategy and make sure that others understand how their jobs, objectives, and rewards relate to the strategy. For people to focus their attention on critical tasks, make effective decisions, concentrate resources, and to maintain and aspire to high standards, they need clear direction. To ensure that the strategy is the right one, a directive leader would press hard for an open, vigorous debate of the economic logic underlying the rationalization proposal. This discussion would illuminate the need for the change and would elicit ideas of how the plan might be modified and improved. Goals cannot be truly shared if they are not understood—and understanding comes from clarity in their expression and specificity about the underlying economic logic. Through forceful action, directive managers ultimately create a consensus in support of goals.

As we have seen, the values-driven leader would take a third approach. Arguing that goals and actions must clearly and consistently reflect and promote the values of the organization, he or she would ensure that the debate also focused on the proposed strategy's effect on the organization's values. For example, standardizing manufacturing might affect the company's ability to serve the customer, to guarantee employment, and to excel in product quality. The values-driven leader would explicitly address and resolve any conflicts, ensure that the strategic decisions reflected this resolution, and inform the organization in such a way that the priority among key values and the reasoning behind the decisions are clearly communicated. The leader's primary concern would be to speak and act in ways that promote and defend critical shared values.

The other two examples described at the beginning of this chapter raise the issue of how managers should deal with the people working for them. In both situations, the political leader would act believing that precision and clarity can be costly or even hazardous. The more specific a leader is, the less latitude subordinates have in their decision making, the less creativity and initiative they employ, and the fewer alternatives they explore and present to senior management. Thus to ensure that the subordinate has thought about the key issues and to show him or her that the manager is concerned, a political leader tends to probe with insightful questions.

The directive leader would look at these two situations as opportunities to identify, analyze, and resolve key issues. Drawing others who could contribute to the issue's resolution into the debate, the manager would encourage open discussion of facts and judgments to arrive at the "best" decision. The leader might allow the subordinate to make the decision, but would make every effort to ensure that it is clear, crisp, and based on sound reasoning. The manager would use the debate to verbally reward the subordinate for revealing the problem. The discussion would result in clear expectations of performance regarding the customer or the equipment investment.

In the last two cases, values-driven leaders would ask what actions would reinforce key values. The values affected might be service to the customer, trust and mutual respect, openness and candor, autonomy, or high-performance standards. For example, when faced with a vague justification for a major investment, values-driven leaders would reassure subordinates that they would become involved if the situation concerned values that mattered to the company, not because they didn't trust others or wanted to take control.

THE PREJUDICE

How should managers approach this dilemma? To achieve outstanding performance, managers should have a strong prejudice toward clear, specific statements of goals as well as behavior that encourages others to pursue clarity and precision as they carry out their own responsibilities. This prejudice is unmistakably an extension of the directive philosophy of leadership, not the political view. By following this prejudice, managers can best achieve consistency among their day-by-day actions and the organizational aims and personal values described in the last chapter.

Consider, for example, the first characteristic of the ideal organization: a shared purpose based on economically viable goals, an innovative vision, high standards, and a sense of community. In practice, each level of an organization works as a filter, distorting and weakening communication. Self-interest, politics, tunnel vision, bureaucracy, conventional wisdom, and daily operating pressures act as prisms to refract and even alter the understanding employees have of the broad purpose and strategy of a company. By erring on the side of clarity and precision, managers increase the chance that others will understand what they are expected to accomplish and will understand the strategy on which they should base their decisions. This prejudice is a critical way of surmounting the difficulties of communicating a strategy to an organization so that it is widely understood and accepted.

Moreover, in a quickly changing, complex world, a bias toward clarity and precision imposes a crucial discipline on managers' thinking about their companies' strategies. As Alexander d'Arbeloff observed, clarity requires the leader to have a sound understanding of his or her business:

> To manage, you really have to understand what you're doing. I've noticed that an awful lot of managers really haven't thought about what they're doing in enough depth; they just follow the dictates of the conventional

wisdom. . . . To make complex issues clear requires the leader to distill the strategy into its key elements and their underlying logic.

Such a distillation forces a manager to establish priorities and crystallize his or her thinking; in the process, a manager often challenges conventional ways of thinking about a company's industry. For example, in explaining the strategy that reshaped the banking industry, Walter Wriston gives this simple account of the underlying logic:

Corporate treasurers had become profit centers. Therefore, the day of the demand, noninterest-earning balance was going the way of the dodo. It was just a question of time before there weren't any. Also, there is a finite amount of money people are going to lend you. Therefore, if you want to be in business in the 1990s, you have to tap the consumer because that is the only place where there is any money. It was a liquidity issue. The funding issue was the cement that held us all together.

Wriston defined Citicorp's strategy in three words: "World financial intermediary." He gave each word a specific meaning. The result was a different way of thinking about the banking business. Through constant exhortation, argument, and cajoling, he made the meaning of these words perfectly clear to Citicorp employees. He reinforced his words through a consistent pattern of actions regarding organizational structure, key personnel, the allocation of human and financial resources, the reward of certain efforts, and the reallocation of responsibilities. Some employees did not like the implications of this new strategy, but they knew what they were expected to do. The result was the successful implementation of a strategy that not only revamped Citibank but also began a revolution in the banking industry.

The political philosophy's justification of vague goals—on the grounds that they increase a manager's flexibility—misses the essence of the issue. It is not the *leader's* flexibility that is of paramount importance, but the flexibility of the *organization* to respond quickly to market changes. Vagueness may give the leader and others more flexibility, but it makes the organization slower to respond to external events. When actions are not focused, subunit goals continue to conflict with the needs of the marketplace realities and the organization moves only slowly into new directions. Particularly in uncertain times, when changes must be made quickly and with little warning, a company needs clear marching orders, not vague goals that others can decipher only over long periods of time. Responsiveness is forged out of a shared understanding of the facts of a situation and the strategy of a company.

Of course, circumstances may limit just how clear and precise a manager can be. One highly successful executive in the electronics industry who faced an environment of declining orders and rapid technological change commented on the different stances he took:

> I was very explicit when sales were going through the roof. So we drove very hard on very specific profitability goals because we could do that. If it's realistic to be clear, be clear. But there are times that, if you are too explicit, you could wreck this place, because in times of high uncertainty nobody can make the trade-offs between short-term and long-term considerations.

Two important assumptions underlie these comments. First, this prejudice, like the others we will describe, is simply that—a prejudice or a bias. It is not a cookie cutter to be stamped on all situations. At times, an outstanding manager will override the prejudice. Second, the right reason for overriding the prejudice is uncertainty about the market, costs, or technology, not considerations of self-interest or internal politics. Even in times of uncertainty, a manager should be as clear as possible. Managers who keep their cards close to their vests risk confusing others and undermining their credibility. The gap between externally and internally generated ambiguity is enormous, and subordinates know it. This difference—an essential distinction between the political and directive philosophies—can have a profound impact on the trust and credibility subordinates vest in their leaders.

Setting Priorities

In arguing for clarity and precision in communicating long-term goals, we are also considering how important it is for employees to have clear guidance about the often conflicting pressures—from the financial community for short-term earnings increases, from customers for more value in the company's products or services, from labor unions for increased wages, and from public bodies for actions that serve their purposes—that a company's many constituencies exert on it.

Managers must balance these pressures, which tend to be immediate, tangible, and measurable in dollars and cents, against the long-term needs for renewing a company's strategy and skills and for sustaining a competitive advantage—factors that ultimately serve all constituents. The long-term competitive position of the company depends on policies and actions whose consequences are less immediate, less certain, and less readily quantifiable. Often they will not take a concrete or tangible form for many years. Unless corporate leaders are clear about which constituency's interests have higher priority, decisions at lower levels in the organization will not reflect an appropriate balance between short- and long-term pressures. Then, short-term financial concerns, by which performance is most commonly measured, dominate other concerns.

James Burke's efforts to revitalize Johnson & Johnson's credo were largely an exercise in establishing priorities among customers, employees, communities in which J&J did business, and shareholders. The final outcome of all the discussions he and President David Clare had with J&J managers about the credo was a renewed understanding and commitment to J&J's fundamental purposes and priorities—a commitment Burke believes was essential to J&J's successful handlings of the Tylenol crisis.

A company facing an intensely competitive global marketplace cannot afford to disperse its resources through unfocused efforts motived by localitis and careerism. A bias toward being clear and specific is much more likely to lead to the concentration of effort and resources that a company requires for success or, in some cases, survival.

When people are clear and specific in three areas—in the facts, values, and assumptions underlying the definition of the problems; in the identification of alternative solutions; and in predictions about the nature of the product/market and organizational forces that affect the outcome of alternative actions—the caliber of their decisions is significantly higher than if they are kept in the dark. By being specific in these three areas, a leader will focus the debate on the substance of the issues, not on personalities or individual stakes in the decision.

Achieving Commitment

Clarity facilitates commitment. The philosophy of values-driven leadership argues that an organization's purposes and values can powerfully motivate employees. They can help them feel that they are serving worthwhile ends and channel their behavior in desired directions. But to have this effect, a company's purpose and values must be clearly articulated and consistently reinforced. It is difficult for a person to commit to a vision that he or she does not comprehend. Normally, vague definitions of purpose are of little value in defining a company's goals. Thus commitment is fundamentally an issue of the integrity of purpose, goals, and action.

Walter Wriston observed that the more talented people are, the more they demand to understand the company's vision and its justification before they will subordinate their self-interests to actions that serve the broader vision.

If you have smart people, they have to be persuaded that what you are doing is reasonable. Therefore, the direction should be made as clear as it can be. If you don't know where you are going, it is hard to get there. If the team doesn't share the goals, you're not going to get there either. It's like giving a speech. You tell them what you are going to tell them, you tell them, and then you tell them what you told them. Then you must act in a way that is consistent with what you have told them.

Consistency in action is vital to the effective communication of a clear vision, goals, and critical values.

Clarity about goals and key assumptions gives the assumptions a visibility that allows subordinates to question them—a process that can lead to greater understanding and ultimately fewer mistakes. Commitment requires understanding.

Expectations, Accountability, and Autonomy

The intellectual strength of a strategy cannot by itself ensure outstanding results. It is the execution of the strategy that separates top performers from the also-rans, and better execution follows from demanding performance standards. To be effective, standards must be clear. With clear goals and expectations, managers can set targets and demand performance that stretches people beyond their current levels of achievement. The challenge of setting such standards is great in itself, without adding the encumbrance of vagueness and generality. Similarly, while performance appraisals are among the more uncomfortable management tasks, they greatly help subordinates' careers and their subsequent performance when they clearly communicate areas needing improvement.

Clear goals and policies, coupled with high standards, reduce the risks that arise when a leader grants considerable operating autonomy to others in the organization. With talented people who agree on basic directions and on the range of acceptable ways these goals can be achieved, managers need fewer intrusive supervisory policies and practices. Furthermore, clarity and precision enhance a company's ability to attract talented people. Such people, who want to make

their marks on a company, seek challenges, fairly adminis-
tered rewards, and autonomy.

Clarity and Trust

Clear objectives and candid feedback on performance, along with a norm of precise communications, can
also help create an atmosphere of trust, in which people know
what they are expected to do and how they will be evaluated.
When everyone can understand what the standards are,
evaluations are more likely to be perceived as fair, not capri-
cious. The detrimental maneuvering that results when performance standards are seen as arbitrary and changing pe-
riodically in response to company politics, rather than
competitive pressures, is substantially reduced. Also, an atmosphere of trust enhances the flow of information through a
company which ensures that top management is not sheltered
from bad news and can respond to new and quickly changing
environments.

Attention to Specifics

Being specific means setting organizational standards
for details. But what should a leader consider a detail? Must a
leader be involved in—or at least aware of—specific operational details of marketing, research, or manufacturing or pay
attention only to actions that will affect the company's basic
values or strategy? Or do leaders mainly make sure that others
pay attention to the details of their jobs?

One CEO gave a vivid example of attending to detail.
On the morning of our meeting with him, as he rode the
elevator, he noticed that a light was out. As soon as he arrived
at his office, before doing anything else, he called to have the
light fixed—and fixed quickly. Fixing the elevator light was
very much a detail, but it was also for him a very important
symbol of a critical value—his company's commitment to excellence.

But leaders must choose carefully what to be specific about and how specific to be. Not all details warrant their attention. To understand this, think about a company as an elaborate hierarchy of objectives, issues, and problems. At its apex are strategic issues that are clearly a leader's responsibility. These issues concern the basic values a company embodies; the contribution it seeks to make to its owners, employees, customers, and the communities in which it does business; the business it is in; the way it secures a competitive advantage in its markets; its economic objectives; and the major functional policies necessary to achieve its goals. At this level, leadership demands clarity in word and deed.

To be effective, however, a strategy must consist of more than statements on paper describing these basic elements. It must shape, every day, the thousands of small decisions made by sales people, first-line supervisors, clerks, and others that cumulatively produce a company's long-term performance. A strategy can influence their efforts only if it is fragmented into increasingly specific and operational objectives. A company's purpose and business concept must shape economic objectives; these must translate into functional goals; functional policies should guide and limit the goals of subunits; these, in turn, break into objectives for task forces and project teams, which are often temporary and focus on something that must be done "this week" or "this quarter." Finally, people must be assigned jobs and develop personal objectives. In Peter Drucker's words, "Strategy must ultimately degenerate into work."

The daily details of implementation are unambiguously the direct responsibility of subordinates. Here, the questions of precision and clarity on the part of the leader do not arise. Leaders delegate considerable autonomy over these operating decisions to subordinates.

In between these two extremes, however, is a gray area in which leaders and others inevitably share responsibility. Here, the prejudice for clarity and precision means that managers must be clear about their expectations and must also demand clear thinking and precise proposals from their subordinates. Even when translated into actions, such expectations are but one step toward successful sharing of responsibility in gray areas. (We look at other gray areas in Chapters 5 and 7, where we consider the dilemmas of top-down versus bottom-up influence and compromise versus conflict.)

A manager who habitually demands clarity and precision in his own thinking and actions sets a powerful example for subordinates, and can demand such thinking from them. Without sustained effort to define important questions precisely and to answer them with specific, detailed evidence and clear, rigorous reasoning, a company and its managers are more likely to drift like a boat without a rudder, guided only by impressions and judgments that no one has thought through. In this vacuum, discussions can shift subtly from issues of external competitiveness to internal politics, from securing product/market advantages to concern about individual interests.

By the same token, a bias toward clarity and precision also imposes a powerful discipline of character. In complex organizations, because expertise is dispersed, power is scattered. As the political philosophy correctly stresses, organizations can break down into separate arenas in which powerful people and groups do battle. Pressing for precision creates a spotlight that can expose and discourage the stratagems of organizational politicians and keep the focus on issues of substance. If subordinates expect that they will have to state and justify their objectives precisely and describe specifically how and when they will achieve them, it is easier for senior managers to be sure their subordinates are pursuing courses of action consistent with their company's strategy, rather than with their self-interests.

Clarity and Integrity

A prejudice for clarity and precision makes a manager's quest for integrity of values, aims, and actions considerably less daunting. Members of an organization are much more likely to understand its basic aims, if these are clearly articulated. They will also know what standards they must meet in their work, the priorities they should follow, and the role of their jobs in accomplishing a company's mission. At the same time, they will better understand their leader's own personal values. When these personal values and basic organizational aims are clearly known, it is easier—though not necessarily easy—for leaders and followers alike to commit themselves to these values and aims and then make decisions and take action that support them. Fundamentally, deep commitment arises from a sense of serving worthwhile ends. Those must be defined and consistently reinforced through a prejudice for clarity and precision in what a manager thinks, says, and does.

Chapter 5

TOP-DOWN VERSUS BOTTOM-UP INFLUENCE

Deciding to what extent they should intervene in subordinates' activities is a problem that managers face daily. Even in small companies, managers must deal with a stream of problems, questions, memos, meetings, and reports through which they could become involved in the decisions and actions of others.

Consider the following situation—one that can easily arise in a small company. You are the president of a successful, $10 million manufacturing company. In the past, you have relied heavily on the judgment of your functional managers. Now, after a thorough, detailed analysis, your vice president for marketing wants to announce a large price increase in your company's major product line. As you think about his analysis and your own sense of the market, you find you disagree. Moreover, you think that the price increase is risky and could lead to problems with several large customers. In the end, however, the difference is fundamentally a judgment call. Whose judgment should prevail?

In large companies, with several levels of management, the problem of top-down versus bottom-up influence becomes even more complicated. For example assume that you are the chairman of a medium-sized bank holding company. In the past, each of your member banks has operated with extraordinary autonomy. Now, deregulation and intensifying competitive pressures are forcing you to consider ways of cutting costs. Among your options is taking the "back office," paper-processing operations out of the local banks and putting them into a large, central operation. Another is to close a few of the local banks that serve adjacent or overlapping areas.

Both moves promise considerable savings. As the chairman and founder of the bank, you created the system of independent local banks. You still believe strongly in your original vision—as do the heads of the local banks. But the president of your holding company and the head of operations are pressing strongly for consolidation and cost control. What would you do? Who should have what influence on this decision?

Finally, assume you are a group president in a large diversified company. A young sales manager, two levels below, speaks to you in the elevator and says she fears that the company is about to lose a major customer because of sloppy after-sale service. You are aware there has been a continuing conflict between the sales and service departments in this division. How should you respond? Should you tell the manager to take up the matter with her boss or should you get involved personally?

In deciding what to do in each of these situations, a manager makes a decision about who should get involved and influence what decisions in a company. Faced with any problem, a manager may draw information and judgments from many levels in the company. In the end, however, some person or group must make a final decision. In organizations with a top-down bias, a single person—or sometimes a small management team—not only sets the company's basic course but also actively directs decisions at lower levels. In contrast, leaders who follow a bottom-up approach give lower-level managers much greater influence over decisions and allow them to make many important decisions themselves.

The top-down versus bottom-up dilemma is unavoidable. All companies, no matter how small, are hierarchies. Various levels of a hierarchy can have more influence or less influence on important decisions. At the heart of this dilemma is the perception that no matter what approach a leader takes there are high potential costs and risks. The central questions a leader faces are threefold. First, who will decide key issues such as setting product/market objectives, choosing critical policies in the company's functional areas, and allocating scarce resources? Second, how will these decisions be made? And third, how will decision making at lower levels be controlled?

The three philosophies of leadership provide very different guidance for managers facing these questions. Hence, they intensify the dilemma of top-down versus bottom-up influence.

Political leadership tilts toward bottom-up decision making. It relies heavily on initiatives from lower levels of an organization to move it in desired directions. A political-minded leader is aware of how important it is for people at lower levels to have a sense of autonomy, control, and initiative. Hence, he or she lets them take the initiative and then acts to shape, guide, and orchestrate their efforts. Even when decisions clearly must be made by the top management team, a political leader relies heavily on subtle, informal processes to guide and influence the decisions of others.

By contrast, directive leadership emphasizes substance, clarity, and confrontation. It leans much more strongly toward top-down influence. When considering whether to get directly and heavily involved in a decision, directive leaders try to distinguish between strategic and tactical decisions. In principle, they want to delegate considerable autonomy over tactical and operating decisions to lower-level managers. But they nevertheless work diligently to maintain their ability to directly influence the decisions their subordinates make, particularly the major ones. Because they prefer substance over process, they are less willing than political leaders to rely on corporate staffs to extend their influence. Instead, they view their ability to influence decisions as coming from open and candid two-way communication and from their own extensive understanding of the business and its decisions. This flow of information and business-specific knowledge encourages a directive leader to probe for potential weaknesses and oversights in proposals developed at lower levels. They are much more directly, forcefully, and fully involved in the activities of their subordinates.

Under values-driven leadership, a company's strong shared values enable a leader to rely more heavily on bottom-up decision making, with the knowledge that shared norms and values will help shape the decisions. Yet values-driven leaders are quick to take direct, personal action on issues in which the company's basic values or strategy are at stake. On these issues, their instincts and behavior resemble those of directive leaders. Otherwise, they prefer to have a company's values shape what others do and decide, rather than get directly involved themselves.

In the three examples cited above, the managers had to choose among specific, practical alternatives. So, we should think about the particulars of each of the three cases, look at the pros and cons of alternative ways of resolving this dilemma, and examine the practical guidance that follows from the three philosophies.

The Case for Bottom-Up Influence.   All three philosophies recognize the value of bottom-up influence on decisions, even though each of them advocates different ways for managers to guide and shape the decisions of their subordinates. The rationale for this common viewpoint is straightforward. Most of what is known and important in a company is not written down; much of it never rises to the top of a company. Companies are, in a sense, hierarchies of wastebaskets: as issues and problems rise to the top levels, more and more detailed information is thrown out along the way.

As managers take on greater and greater responsibility, they know less and less about the details of what happens below them. They inevitably rely more and more heavily on people at lower levels, who are closer to customers, operating problems, technology, and personnel issues. Moreover, most progress in companies occurs in small steps, taken by people working on small issues, at lower levels of a company. Most good ideas, as Walter Wriston observed, come from someone other than the leader.

Bottom-up influence makes it much easier to attract talented individuals. They can be given authority, responsibility, and accountability. And with clear accountability and responsibility, it is much easier to base promotions on genuine merit. Moreover, it makes little sense for a leader to talk about his faith in the abilities of others and not give them the chance to show what they can do.

The values-driven philosophy of leadership provides the final reason for preferring strong bottom-up influence. By giving others freedom of action and by encouraging them to exercise their own creativity and initiative, a leader raises the chances that people will find personal fulfillment in their work. As people come to believe that they can make decisions that make a difference, their work becomes more meaningful. They have the sense of serving a worthwhile purpose (a purpose that they have helped to choose) and feel that through their work they can realize more of their potential as human beings. The result is improved motivation, enhanced loyalty to an organization's purpose, and more focused decision making.

This bottom-up orientation does not mean, however, that a leader merely reacts to others' initiatives. Quite the contrary. A leader must provide the strategic vision that brings a focus to, and creates criteria for evaluating, bottom-up ideas. Sometimes, of course, if other managers are pursuing clearly inappropriate goals and policies, if a sound strategy is being badly implemented, if customer complaints occur, or if performance measures decline period after period, a manager must intervene and override any preference for bottom-up decision making. Decisions that strongly influence a company's strategic direction or affect a company's basic values also call for a manager's intervention. Genuine bottom-up influence is evidence of mutual trust and respect, both of which are central to the personal values and organizational aims that underlie leadership. Finally, if a manager has succeeded in making his or her vision for an organization clear, it should not be necessary to intervene as frequently or as directly in what others are doing.

The Heart of the Dilemma.   Unfortunately, a leader could not resolve the three problems described at the beginning of this chapter by acting upon a simple preference for bottom-up influence, nor would top-down intervention work. In all three cases, the issues fall in gray areas. It is often unclear whether a decline in some performance indicator is serious enough to warrant action, whether conflicts among subordinates on an issue are excessive or dominated by self-interest, or whether a departure from established practices really threatens basic values or competitive strengths.

For example, the bank chairman who had to decide whether to pursue cost savings through consolidation had a difficult time determining whether costs were the whole issue or even the central issue at stake. If cost had been the only issue, the situation would hardly have been a dilemma. If the holding company could cut its expenses by creating one large back office and by closing several of its operations, then it should do so. But in this case, the chairman of the bank had recruited dozens of young, talented MBAs and promised them the chance to run their own banks. To provide opportunities for those he had already recruited, and to continue successful recruiting in the future, he needed a bank with an image of growth, not consolidation and retreat. Moreover, he had worked hard to build a positive, progressive image in his community and an entrepreneurial culture within the bank, and these would also be undercut by shutting down operations. Finally, the chairman believed that "cutting costs is always the easiest way out of a problem." His strong conviction was that his organization should work harder to find customers, to build assets, and to provide services whose fees covered the cost of operations. At the same time, his top management team could clearly see the intense cost pressures that deregulation could impose on their business.

Who, then, should influence the decision about consolidation? A simple bottom-up preference would give the presidents of the local banks a license to follow their natural tendency to oppose consolidation. On the other hand, since they were closest to their markets and potential customers, the local presidents were in the best position to judge whether growth or consolidation was the more attractive course.

Similarly, the episode we described at the beginning of this chapter involving the possible loss of a major customer because of sloppy after-sale service also falls in a gray area. No manager wants to lose an important customer, particularly through mediocre service. Yet the responsibility for problems of this kind rests several levels lower in the organization. If managers get directly involved, they can easily reduce others' accountability for their actions, lower the degree of trust between levels of management, undercut the authority of managers in between, and even reduce the willingness of others to take risks. Because it is so difficult to weigh the effects of such secondary consequences, it is even more difficult for managers to determine whether and how to intervene in gray area situations.

The Achilles' Heel.   Subordinates, especially aggressive and entrepreneurial ones, can dissipate company resources and depart from the company's strategy and the leader's personal values and aspirations. Once power is dispersed to many autonomous units, it is much more difficult for companies to respond to major changes. A decentralized system can, of course, effect small incremental changes. But major changes that affect the organization as a whole, which usually have major implications for the incumbent managers, are unlikely to well up from the bottom.

Greater autonomy and bottom-up influence have other negative consequences that advocates of decentralization and local entrepreneurship often overlook. With local autonomy, top management and staff have considerably less control over a company's operations. Autonomy can also improve the establishment of standard practices and prevent a company from achieving economies of scale and standardization. Companies may find it much harder to concentrate resources on carefully defined and limited targets. The forces driving bottom-up influence can also become so splintered that resources are spread too thinly, efforts are duplicated, and expertise and costs are not shared across businesses.

The executive team of the bank holding company facing the issue of consolidation had all of these risks in mind. Was the bank growing too fast and in too many directions? Was it dispersing its resources so widely that its individual products and markets would be vulnerable to attack by focused competitors? Were duplicate activities at many of the autonomous local banks raising costs unnecessarily? And were the local bank presidents, each pursuing the interests of his or her own unit, failing to learn as much as they could from each other?

The Case for a Top-Down Approach. All of these factors provide a rationale for strong central guidance of a company. Central guidance and control are ways of countering localitis and the other splintering forces that crop up in most companies. The executive faced with the problem of sloppy service surely asked himself whether his company as a whole was not suffering because two subunits, marketing and service, were fighting a battle of local baronies. Moreover, from an economic and competitive point of view, companies must often use systems and structures to eliminate peripheral activities and concentrate resources on a few carefully chosen strategic goals.

Strong values that are widely shared—the essence of values-driven leadership—also rein in fragmenting forces. Employees throughout a company should have a common understanding of how to approach decisions. The marketing vice president, insisting on a large, unilateral price increase, one that could jeopardize a major customer, had raised problems that could affect the rest of the company. If the company lost the customer, its cash flow would be diminished (which would limit its ability to make further investments), its plant would run under capacity, layoffs might be necessary, and inventory costs could rise. These were strong reasons for the president of the company to intervene, reexamine, and perhaps even reject the proposed price increase.

In this light, the tension between top-down and bottom-up influence becomes part of a much broader dilemma: the tension between management practices that bring strategic focus to company activities, on the one hand, and the importance of encouraging entrepreneurship and autonomy, on the other. On the side of centralization are many of the concepts, techniques, attitudes, and systems designed to produce a focused, cohesive corporate strategy and a rational, efficient allocation of resources that supports the strategy. On balance, these exert strong, centralizing forces on a company. They are the tools of direct top-down influence. During the 1970s, as managers adopted and then perfected many of these techniques for strategic planning and resource allocation, the centralizing and controlling forces became stronger and stronger. This led to a widespread criticism of the planning, controlling, centralizing mentality. Many argued that it had handicapped U.S. companies, making them less competitive, and, in particular, undermining their ability to innovate.

The various rationales for top-down influence all exert pressure in the same direction: toward *managing* risk rather than *taking* risk; toward shared beliefs and practices rather than challenges to conventional wisdom; and often toward short-term financial measures of performance rather than long-term, less quantifiable standards and objectives. As the rationales for central control and direction grow stronger, all the benefits of bottom-up influence and local autonomy are imperiled.

Doing Nothing as an Option.   The top-down versus bottom-up dilemma, and the difficulties gray areas pose, are exacerbated by another factor: the difficulty of deciding whether doing nothing at all would be a more effective approach. In thinking through a "do nothing" or "do nothing now" scenario, a manager must consider several questions: What chain of events is likely to occur if I take no action? Who else is likely to act? What will they do? How sound will the thinking underlying their decision be? What role will company politics play? What values will shape the decision and its implementation?

Nonintervention can be as dramatic and eventful as vigorous action: it can signal powerfully what a manager's true priorities are and how he or she prefers to handle situations. Doing nothing also provides several other advantages. First, it keeps decisions at the organizational level with the most information about products and markets. Second, it can keep managers from intervening when they lack the skill, time, or power to act successfully. Third, since doing nothing usually means that others will do something, it gives a manager opportunities to learn more about peers' and subordinates' skills, values, and interests.

On the other hand, if a manager does nothing, others are likely to fill the vacuum. In the case of the bank considering consolidation, if the CEO didn't intervene, the other members of the executive team, who favored consolidation, were likely to clash with the individual bank presidents who preferred to continue the past policy of growth. By not acting, the CEO could secure the advantages of bottom-up influence described in the last section. By delegating the decision to others, however, he would greatly reduce his influence on the final outcome. The same holds true in the other two examples. If the marketing manager went ahead with the price increase he proposed, the company president might preserve his credibility and have the opportunity to learn more about the judgment of his marketing head. But the price change might put the organization at risk. And if the executive questioned about sloppy service did not get involved, he would get a much clearer idea of how well the people who work for him could resolve the problem, but he could also lose customers unnecessarily.

Nonintervention raises two general issues, one minor and one major. The smaller issue lies in the expectations a senior manager creates when he or she chooses not to get involved. Others will expect that in similar situations in the future the same pattern will hold, that they will have the prerogative to decide on their own. Such precedents and expectations can limit a senior executive's options. But the greater issue, by far, is that gray area situations by their very nature involve strong reasons why a manager *should* get involved. It is in the gray areas where leaders have the greatest opportunities to set standards and clarify intentions.

THE PREJUDICE

What advice can best guide managers who must find ways to balance top-down and bottom-up influence on important decisions?

Managers can resolve this dilemma best if they try to extend their capacities to exert direct top-down influence, but limit sharply how frequently they exercise this capacity. That is, managers should try to eliminate the barriers and filters that limit their ability to experience, understand, and influence decisions at lower levels in an organization. They need to understand, as much as possible, what is going on below them. But at the same time, they must limit how often they take direct action. Instead, their overriding concern should be to develop strong leaders, whether middle managers or functional heads, who can take direct action on their own. This is more than simply a prejudice for approaching specific situations. It has profound implications for a company's formal structure and systems as well as for the formal and informal delegation of responsibility.

A manager's ability and readiness to intervene in a top-down, direct way is an essential condition for granting autonomy to subordinates. This idea is paradoxical but fundamental. Autonomy means that a central office, senior manager, or powerful corporate staff will not second-guess what operating managers do. Autonomy and bottom-up influence mean that line officers have the opportunity to make decisions and take action as they see fit.

But substantial autonomy inevitably means that they will have the opportunity to make errors, potentially very damaging ones. Managers must know when their subordinates are in situations in which the risk of a serious mistake or error is high. They need not act in each of these situations, but they

must know when these situations occur so that they can decide whether or not to act. And, when it becomes clear that a
serious error is likely to occur, it is imperative that senior
executives be able to act quickly and decisively to head it off.
They must be able to intervene effectively and quickly—and
this means strong top-down action.

   Maintaining a Top-Down Capacity.   But what does
it mean, in practice, for managers to maintain their capacity
for top-down influence, while encouraging operating autonomy? In the first place, it means that leaders must use a variety
of tools—including probing questions on key strategic issues—to assure themselves that their operating managers have
both a personal feel and a clear understanding of their markets
and the critical trends that will shape the future of their businesses.

   Second, there is no substitute for senior executives
who know the businesses and operations reporting to them
from firsthand experience. Businesses cannot be run simply
by the numbers. Almost without fail, operating managers have
testified to the difference between the intellectual understanding they had of the business before they took charge of it and
the visceral, intuitive, experienced-based feeling they have for
a business after they have run it for several years. Knowing a
business permits senior executives to read between the lines
of performance reports and to ask critical questions about possible trouble areas. It also gives them a much better ability to
assess the answers they get. As a result, in a much shorter time
and without the appearance of direct, intrusive intervention,
they can sense whether a manager who is operating with considerable autonomy is on or off track.

   Hubie Clark, CEO of Baker International, described
this concern:

   The general manager's [whether divisional or corporate]
   prime obligation is to "feel" his business—to have a sensitivity to the market trends and geopolitical forces that
   will impact his market. If you don't sense where the mar-

ket is going, then all else can be lost. This sense needs to be a very personal one, and it is difficult to achieve working through a staff.

Clark believed that when problems arose in the divisions, he should opt for autonomy rather than intercede directly in decision making. He explained:

> When you start to get involved in divisional decision making, it is certain death. You cannot ever extract yourself. When a management problem arises, we try—as long as we feel safe—to encourage, train, and enhance the people that are there. We never remove their decision-making authority.

Despite Clark's belief, on occasion Baker managers were replaced if they could not focus their attention and understand the critical trends in their markets, or if there was clear evidence that the division had outgrown a person's managerial abilities.

A further, broad implication of this experience-based approach is that leaders seeking outstanding performance must limit the range of businesses and products that their companies pursue. Otherwise, only superhuman executives can have a genuine, thorough command of the facts and subtle operating issues. As it is, the greater the range of businesses and products, and the greater their complexity, the more likely it is that management by numbers will supplant management by experience.

Maintaining the capacity for top-down influence also means following the first prejudice: being clear and precise in one's own actions and expecting clarity and precision from subordinates. When clear, mutually acceptable performance standards are in place, it is easier to spot possible problem areas. Benchmarks for performance of functional heads and business unit managers need not be short-term, financial criteria. They can reflect long-term factors and uncertainty. The key point is that clear markers indicate when a manager or a unit may be going astray. If these are in place, intervention need only occur on an exception basis.

Personal Attitudes.   The executives we interviewed saw the ability to get good information as critical to maintaining their capacities for effective top-down influence. Most strongly emphasized that they did not penalize subordinates who brought them bad news. The president of one company said that the only person in the business who was not permitted to make mistakes was his helicopter pilot. In contrast, delaying bad news was considered a serious offense. However, to sustain the pressure for bottom-up influence and prevent responsibility and accountability from gravitating upward, most CEOs whom we interviewed did not look favorably on subordinates who brought problems to them without at the same time bringing ideas for solving them.

When they met with their subordinates, the leaders we interviewed tried to avoid signalling their own opinions prematurely. Instead, they asked others to give their views of the situation. They were well aware that when the boss speaks, everyone listens and many follow, frequently without thinking. Often, it was quite difficult to show restraint. One executive said that he sometimes had to literally keep a finger on his mouth to discourage himself from saying how he thought a problem or situation should be handled.

Preferring to hear subordinates' views first does not mean being cautious or vague about one's own views. Most of the leaders we talked to stressed the importance of being open and candid and of confronting difficult issues rather than postponing them. Most had "open door" policies, which they viewed as a way to limit the filters at lower levels in the organization. Richard Munro commented, "If one of the people I work with has a problem, they come in here and we talk about it. That's not a problem." He stressed that he "campaigned" for openness, spending an enormous amount of time on this effort.

Being clear about one's own view includes acknowledging the occasions when one is unsure; it even extends to admitting error. Efforts to maintain a facade of infallibility generally don't fool shrewd people for very long. Acknowledging that one has made mistakes makes it easier for subordinates to acknowledge their own uncertainties and errors. In the same vein, an attitude that reflects a genuine desire to learn and to understand how the world looks from the perspective of subordinates is far less threatening than an aggressive, interrogating style. The latter simply promotes fear, which in turn encourages managers to hide errors, mask uncertainties, and suppress questions whose answers may be quite important.

No formulas, guidelines, or even prejudices can answer the question of whether a leader should intervene in a particular gray area situation. The leaders we interviewed had only two general pieces of advice in such cases. First, they relied, in the end, on their own gut instincts; second, on the advice of trusted advisers. These advisers can be board members, executives in other companies, the leader's predecessor, or a trusted lower-level executive. What characterizes the best of these advisers is that they "have been there before." They have worked on, resolved, or even failed at times to handle gray area situations. Discussing the situation with them and paying careful attention to their advice does not guarantee a right answer about the best timing for direct intervention. It does, however, load the dice in favor of better judgments in situations in which top-down and bottom-up influence must be balanced.

Intervention and Integrity

The daily quest for integrity requires that a manager be able to intervene, sometimes decisively, in order to keep a company or a department on course, to translate a vision and demanding standards into reality, to prevent others from making serious mistakes, to grant autonomy to others while acknowledging ultimate responsibility for what they do, and to penetrate the filters and buffers that inevitably clog organizations. Yet repeated, forceful intervention in others' work and responsibilities can discourage high-caliber people because they don't want to be "yes men." It can diminish ethical standards by implying that managers don't trust or respect the people working for them; it is hardly a way for a leader to express his or her faith in others' talents. It also moves decisions away from the people closest to customers and operations. For all these reasons, a manager's effort to achieve integrity through daily action requires a strong capability for top-down intervention tempered by a strong preference for bottom-up influence.

Chapter 6

SUBSTANCE VERSUS PROCESS

A third classic dilemma is the tension between substance and process. In its simplest terms, managers face this dilemma when they have to decide between working directly to get the right answer to a problem and working on the right way of getting the answer. It is the conflict between emphasizing the "what" and the "how" of making decisions.

Faced with any specific problem, a manager could choose to address the substance of the problem—personally focusing attention and effort on data, analysis, and judgments that will help produce the right answer to the problem. Or, taking a significantly different approach, a manager could concentrate on the way in which other people gather information, conduct analysis, and reach conclusions. Instead of concentrating directly on the problem, a manager tries to enable others to make the right decisions by shaping the informal as well as the formal processes—the organizational structures and the planning, control, information, and compensation systems—that influence how others will make a decision. A manager may make no effort to determine the answer to the problem, but instead may specify who will be responsible for dealing with it, how they should proceed, the objectives that should guide their decisions, and what will be rewarded.

To gain a better understanding of this dilemma, think about three situations.

First, assume that you are the CEO of a company in an industry with rapid technological change. Your research and engineering departments report to a vice president of R&D, who is one of the most respected and valuable people in the company. You know there are many disputes among sales, R&D, and manufacturing personnel over the design and timeliness of new products and the updating of current ones.

Sales and manufacturing complain that R&D sends products into production too early. Manufacturing charges that engineering does not check the drawings closely enough. (R&D makes over one thousand production changes per year.) R&D argues that they are under intense pressure from sales to rush products to market, that manufacturing doesn't cooperate during the design phase, and that sales is lax in communicating customer needs to R&D. Your company has regular executive committee meetings of top management for communicating routine information and addressing everyday problems. The executive committee meets tomorrow. What action would you take to resolve these problems?

Second, as a group vice president of a diversified company, you are responsible for five strategic business units (SBUs). With the help of one of the country's most respected management consulting firms, corporate management has just put a new strategic planning process in place. The CEO has worked hard to implement it and you have supported him. The new system created twenty-four SBUs, each of which has been classified on the basis of its position in the product life cycle and the attractiveness of its industry. The system's basic aim is to have capital flow from the aged businesses to the embryonic and growth businesses. You have worked very hard to get your business units to understand their roles in the new approach. Particularly with the mature and aging businesses, this has not been easy: before, they weren't under pressure to generate cash flow. One of the five strategic business units reporting to you is the commodity water-treatment chemicals business. It is classified as a mature business in a stagnant industry. Yet its manager has proposed an investment in a new plant as part of a major thrust in the sun-belt region. His plan promises attractive returns and future growth—yet it runs directly counter to the business's role in the new planning system and corporate strategy. What do you do?

Third, assume it is six years later and you have just been made CEO of this same company. You think that the planning process is no longer as effective as it once was or as it could be. The collective strategies of the SBUs do not add up to a cohesive corporate strategy and your company is not innovating as rapidly as competitive conditions require for continued market leadership. This is happening despite a significant increase in the size of the planning staffs in the company, the development of comprehensive strategic plans by each SBU, and annual reviews of each business unit's strategy by the major corporate officers, the relevant group vice president, and key managers of the business unit. What actions would you consider?

The three philosophies would prescribe very different approaches for resolving these problems. In each situation, a political-minded leader would be less inclined to get directly involved in the substance of the problems—because it is the responsibility of others to work them out—and would instead try to alleviate problems and influence outcomes by changing organization structures and systems that affect their decisions. A political leader would also work on immediate problems through careful, subtle, behind-the-scenes orchestration of the formal and informal processes of the company. Political-minded leaders care, of course, that the right decisions be made. But they also see themselves as realists. They know the limits of what one manager can do, and they know that a company's "processes" have a vast influence on when and how others make decisions.

In the situation involving guerrilla warfare among R&D, manufacturing, and sales, the political philosophy would advise the CEO to be very careful in the executive committee meeting about expressing his own thinking, except in general terms. This is so that he will not prejudice the discussion, will maintain his flexibility, and, above all, in view of the self-interests of the individuals and departments involved, be able to seize opportunities to guide key managers to solutions that are likely to make some progress on the problem. During the meeting and afterward, he would seek opportunities to change the organization structure and compensation systems in ways that would encourage greater cooperation among the three departments. (For example, by creating project manager positions to act as an integrator across functions on new products, or rewarding managers for successful cooperation with other departments.) He might also ask representatives from each functional area to work as a task force on the problem.

In the second case, a political leader's predisposition would be to defend the strategic planning process as more important to the whole company than the water-treatment chemical investment opportunity. If exceptions are made for this SBU, it would set a precedent for the other SBUs to argue for special considerations. This would undermine the hard-won adherence to the new planning system and the benefits that flow from it.

In the third example, the case of the disappointing planning system, a political leader would be inclined to seek a solution through changes in the formal planning process, by modifying incentive compensation to motivate more cohesion among the SBU plans, or by modifying the organization structure. In the late 1970s, General Electric faced a similar dilemma. Reginald Jones, then GE's CEO, had spent nearly a decade building and refining General Electric's strategic planning systems. But he lamented that diverse plans were causing the "balkanization" of GE. In addition, the plans themselves had become so thick that there wasn't enough time for him to read them. But the plans did have to be read and approved. Jones added that, at first glance, "the reports were so persuasive that you'd sign up for everything." His solution was to create another organizational level, sectors, to review the SBU plans. The six sectors grouped the SBUs into related industries. It was the responsibility of the sector manager to integrate his SBUs' plans into a cohesive strategy at the industry level. Jones then could focus on creating cohesion among the six sector strategies. He also created powerful incentives for making the sectors work by placing his potential successors at the head of the sectors. The horse race for the top job helped ensure the sector heads' attention to the cohesion issue.

Directive leaders are much more concerned with the final decisions than with the process leading to them. They are driven to get directly involved in decisions, to try hard to get the right decision made, and to ensure that process is not part of the problem. They act directly and openly, not subtly and behind-the-scenes. They want to set an example for others and to be sure that others understand what they think. They use formal processes to get and communicate information, to make responsibilities, standards, and rewards clear, and to maintain control over a company. Because they want candor and decisions based on strategy and economics to dominate decisions in a company, they also care about informal processes. For them, changes in formal processes are clearly a supplemental means of reinforcing the leader's direct attack on the substance of the issue.

In the first situation, even if it made people at the meeting uncomfortable or prompted tempers to flare, a directive leader would make sure that the charges and countercharges among the functional areas were put on the table for open and candid debate. He or she would shift the focus of the debate from emotions and parochial interests to the substantive issues underlying the disputes. The aim of the meeting would be to get solutions based on the merit of the different arguments, regardless of whose ox might be gored. If necessary, the leader would conduct further meetings of the same sort until the problem was solved, and then follow up tenaciously to be sure the decisions were implemented.

In the situation in which the chemical treatment investment contradicted the planning system, a directive leader would think about the problem more in terms of its effect on strategy, sales, profits, and returns rather than in terms of the integrity of the planning system. He or she would focus on the competitive substance of this decision, not the larger process surrounding it. Rigid rules are earmarks of bureaucracy.

A directive leader facing the cumbersome planning system would be inclined to streamline and simplify it, perhaps dramatically, to prevent process from driving out substance in the formulation of strategy. He or she would cut back staff involvement and instead get personally involved in judging and influencing the SBUs' strategies and the caliber of the thinking behind them. The leader would push forward with questions like these: What are the competitors doing? How might they respond? Do you have the people and resources to achieve our goals?

Directive leaders want to hear focused strategies and plans from their subordinates, not read elaborate plans and their documentation. This was Jack Welch's, Jones's successor, approach at GE. Welch took strong action to reduce what he thought were planning rituals that had begun to debilitate the company's strategic decision-making processes. For Welch, the solution rested in increasing the focus on substance, simplifying the planning process, reducing the role of staff, and increasing the direct involvement of the CEO in the strategy formulation process. He eliminated one layer of planning review—the sector level—and personally reviewed the SBU plans. Further, he dramatically cut the number of people attending the plan review meetings. Only the three members of the chief executive office (Welch and the two vice chairmen) and the SBU managers attended the new review meetings. No longer were GE's plan review sessions conducted with what Welch called "robes and incense."

For values-driven leaders, strategy is more than just maximizing economic performance; process matters vitally. These leaders care deeply that values such as cooperation, trust, mutual respect, creativity, and individual freedom and autonomy shape what people in a company do and think. Such values must come into play, and are often at risk, when tough decisions must be made. Reinforcing these values matters more to these leaders than the question of whether they should be directive or political. Whether they get directly involved or not depends, in part, on whether the situation at hand threatens their company's core values or provides a chance to strengthen them.

In the case involving the clashing functional areas, a values-driven leader would remind everyone, at the very outset, of their shared commitment to competitive excellence and to cooperation, trust, mutual respect, and openness in trying to solve their problems. Whether he became directly involved or not would then depend on whether the people at the meeting worked in accord with these values and whether the decisions emerging from their work were consistent with them. Since he would see this situation as an opportunity to defend and reinforce these values, which are clearly threatened in this situation, it is likely that he would be active.

In the case of the deviant investment proposal, a values-driven leader would be likely to see the values of creativity, individual initiative, and autonomy at stake. As such, he or she would be very concerned about how a decision—especially one that seemed to subordinate these values to the planning process—would affect these values and the signals it would send to employees throughout the company.

Similarly, in trying to fix the deficient planning system, a values-driven leader would try to make candor, confrontation, and openness the dominant values guiding company planning. For example, largely by personal example and direct involvement, Jack Welch set out to reinforce the values of openness and "constructive conflict" in GE's decision-making process. When conflicts were not openly discussed, he would stop meetings specifically to address the reasons for the lack of candor.

The Heart of the Dilemma

Why are there such conflicting views—even among outstanding leaders like Reginald Jones and Jack Welch—about the right way to handle situations in which substance and process collide? The answer is this: managing process is inescapably part of a manager's job, yet process, both formal and informal, creates some of the most serious risks a manager faces.

This dilemma was not a concern for the many tiny, owner-managed companies that dominated the U.S. economy early in the last century, nor is it a threat today for the managers of very small companies. These managers must, of course, be concerned about the informal ways in which their employees work with one another and make decisions, but

they have such hands-on involvement in day-to-day operations that they don't need to work through formal processes or
detailed organizational structures and complex management
systems. But modern capitalism is also large-scale managerial
capitalism. Many managers must guide the actions of hundreds or even thousands of people through formal measurement and reward systems, through budgeting and planning
systems, and through the many social and political processes
that link employees of a company.

These managers have no choice: managing process is
part of the substance of their jobs. Systems and processes can
shape the context in which subordinates make decisions and
guide others toward decisions that are consistent with the
company's strategy. This enables managers who are closer to
customers and operations to decide just how to implement the
strategy, giving senior executives the time to concentrate on
broader and longer-term issues. Furthermore, with good systems, senior managers can grant more autonomy to other managers.

Good systems can also spread information about
what is happening in a company, help managers oversee
their subordinates, and encourage fair and consistent decisions throughout a company because everyone is playing by
the same rule book. The right formal management process is
often a substantive solution to a problem. Organization structure can determine whether someone has the right information to make a decision. Compensation systems are powerful
motivators and directors of behavior.

Moreover, leaders of every philosophy care about and
work on informal processes. A political leader often views the
informal process as a means of guiding other managers. For
directive leaders, informal processes determine whether decisions are made in a bureaucratic manner or through debate
focused on issues. They also know that healthy informal processes mean that they can run a company effectively with a
minimal level of formal systems and structures. And values-
driven leaders know that informal processes are the daily,
fundamental test of whether a company affects the way people
treat each other and make decisions.

Managers then are inescapably immersed in process. This fact is reflected in the results of an intensive study of the way twelve successful general managers thought about their work. It concluded:

> The primary focus of on-line managerial thinking is on organizational and interpersonal processes. By "process" I mean the way managers bring people and groups together to handle problems and take action. Whether proposing a change in the executive compensation structure, establishing priorities for a diverse group of business units, consolidating redundant operations, or preparing for plant closings, a senior executive's conscious thoughts are foremost on the processes for accomplishing a change or important decision: "Who are the key players here, and how can I get their support? Whom shall I talk to first? Should I start by getting the production group's input? What kind of signal will that send to the marketing people?"[1]

The Risks of Process

Unfortunately, because process matters so much to managers, they may overlook its dangers. The administrative processes of a company can feed on themselves, grow ever more elaborate, and eventually triumph over substance. When this occurs, the consequences for institutional integrity and performance can be grave. Abraham Zaleznik, a long-time student of executive leadership, has warned that:

> Politicization occurs in business when substance takes a back seat to process—when people become preoccupied with how to relate to each other rather than with what the relationship is supposed to accomplish. Perhaps without realizing what they are doing, managers shift the content of their communication from working on tasks to working on other people's heads. Under the real conditions of inequality of power, which is characteristic of organizations, this shift in communication tyrannizes

people and leads to defensive behavior. Politics in business is a game of defense. But what people are defending against is seldom revealed in the effort to adhere to a superficial ideology of cooperation and teamwork.[2]

Even if it does not politicize a company, relying on "working the process" to influence desired behavior often has disappointing results. It is only an indirect way to influence others. Often, it is about as satisfying and effective as pushing on a string. The effects of new systems and structures on the actions of others can fall far short of the effort required to create and implement them. Moreover, their effects are often unpredictable. Most managers can give painful examples of the unintended consequences of changes to compensation systems. As Walter Wriston observed, "People with the ingenuity to build the Hoover Dam can figure out ways to beat the Hay [compensation] System."

The standard operating procedures developed to guide and shape decision making can take on a life of their own, unrelated to the substance of the issues at hand. As they are adapted to unforeseen situations, and as more and more data are gathered to improve the accuracy and fairness of allocation decisions, they grow more complex. Also, making systems more elaborate can become an intriguing intellectual challenge for those who are responsible for designing them. In order to do their work more effectively and expand their personal influence, they often press to expand the systems and demand more information.

At General Electric, Jack Welch identified another critical problem associated with vibrant corporate staffs, composed of intelligent, well-meaning individuals—their lack of direct responsibility:

> One problem with the staff the way it has been is that the staff has staff in production, in technology, and so on. They then come in as a peer to sit and review something, but are never called on to belly-up. They don't have to come up with a yes or no.[3]

The result can be advice and criticism from the staff, given with impunity, that line managers see as restrictive, intrusive controls, rather than helpful advice. The more creative the line manager's idea, and, therefore, the more uncertain the outcomes, the more staff scrutiny and criticism it can elicit.

Reliance on systems to influence others can be seductive for other reasons as well. With emotionally charged, contentious issues, the path of least resistance is often to "let the system resolve it." Also, systems and self-interest interact. When personal stakes in a situation are high, people use systems, and seek changes in them, to protect their own interests and avoid direct and often unpleasant confrontations.

Finally, because most systems become standardized and are applied across the board, they are by their very nature inexact, and can result in unfair consequences. Furthermore, complexity creates a bias toward bureaucracy and motivates people to create more elaborate organizational processes. For example, when personnel are rewarded—as they often are—based on how many people they manage or the number of activities for which they are responsible, and not for their performance or the contribution of their units to the company, they are simply encouraged by the system to add personnel and activities.

The president of a major media company described clearly how the mechanics and ritual of process can triumph over substance. He explained that his company had lost nearly $100 million on a misguided venture. He tried to figure out "how we managed to study something for a year and screw it up to a degree that was unbelievable." He learned that several division managers in closely related businesses had had serious reservations about the project but had not voiced them. Why? The president offered this explanation:

> They got overwhelmed by the b.s. and the analysis and the slides. We're very good at that, especially the slides. The rules should be less . . . slides and more questions. You leave one of our presentations and you're dazzled by it. You think, "Gee, how can I ask any questions.

They seem to have thought of everything." And yet, we had people who knew deep in their souls it wasn't going to work.

Even when presentations and plans are not dazzling, their sheer size and number can make it very hard for executives to distill their substance. Moreover, the formality of the presentations can obscure the important issues. An outstanding entrepreneur we interviewed echoes this in his complaint:

> I just get nothing out of these formal strategy review meetings. People mouth conventional wisdom. You learn nothing that you didn't know before you went in. Why do I have to go and sleep through these things?

Another major risk of emphasizing process is that it can encourage self-interest and localitis in decision making. Consider, for example, the resource allocation process. Healthy business and functional units inevitably compete for resources to ensure their own growth. Funding and staffing decisions create winners and losers, and they can greatly enhance or severely constrain managers' careers. As a result, the resource allocation process can become an elaborate political arena in which managers seek to defend their personal interests and those of their units. In the battle for capital, a manager may submit overly optimistic projections to show that a particular project clears the corporate hurdle rate of return. Because all projections deal with uncertainty and are based on product/market information that the functional or business units know best, it is often difficult for corporate management to evaluate the accuracy of projections that originate with experts several levels below them in the organization. In response to politically tainted information, senior managers often institute more detailed and elaborate systems and increase the number of checks and balances. The result is the further growth of formal process. Each new attempt to limit or rein in the forces of localitis stimulates further efforts to surmount the new limits. Process begets process, and substance becomes increasingly imperiled.

THE PREJUDICE

No leader, regardless of his or her philosophy, likes bureaucracy or wants process to dominate. These threaten a manager's effort to reconcile the personal values and organization aims that are central to integrity and leadership. With too much emphasis on process, decision making slows, and creativity ebbs: communication becomes less open as it goes through more layers and filters, high-caliber talent is frustrated, trust erodes, politics spiral. But without enough process, a company will fly apart. And unless it is very small, no manager can hold a company together simply by direct personal effort.

A useful prejudice must recognize and reconcile all these conflicting factors. Hence, when substance and process collide, a manager should first set a clear personal example of focusing directly on issues of substance. Second, he or she must manage the formal and informal processes in a company with a central objective: keeping others focused on the substance of their tasks. H. Ross Perot, the founder of Electronic Data Systems Corporation, one of the world's premier systems integration companies, captured the essence of this prejudice with the observation that one of his foremost objectives at EDS was "to create an environment in which people spend every minute of every day doing productive work."

The rationale for a strong prejudice toward substance is clear: the tendency for process—in any of its forms—to dominate substance imperils everything that characterizes a first-class company. The most powerful way a manager can counter the erosion of substance by process is through personal example. The reason is simple: example is the strongest, most convincing form of communication. The priorities revealed in a manager's actions tend to be replicated at lower levels of the business. For this reason, it is important for a manager to display a preoccupation with substantive business issues, not the mechanics of analytical techniques or the niceties of procedure.

Knowledge of the Business

To display a preoccupation with substance, a manager must know the business. Of course, a manager cannot know all the operating details of various functional areas. Some of these details—especially in high-technology R&D— require recent, advanced knowledge in specialized areas. But a leader must understand the basic economics of the business, the recurring operating problems that it faces, the skills and limitations of its managers, and its competitive position within the industry. In this context, understanding means much more than having a cursory acquaintance based largely on reports and studies. Ideally, it means that a manager has had operating responsibility for some aspect of the business or direct responsibility for running a similar business. It also means a manager has spent enough time in charge of a business to work through both the ups and downs of its markets and through several significant operating problems.

This insistence on understanding is, at first glance, simple common sense. Yet it also runs counter to much conventional wisdom. It implies—quite correctly—that "professional managers" can rarely move from business to business or industry to industry carrying kits of techniques and be as effective as a comparably trained manager who knows his or her business in depth. To be sure, there may be an elite cadre of managers whose intellect, experience, and savvy enable them to migrate successfully from business to business or to manage extremely diversified companies with success. But they are the exception, not the rule, and they can come near grief before succeeding.[4]

What is the value of direct familiarity with a business? Before answering this question, consider what familiarity does not provide. It does not enable a manager to give detailed directions to subordinates. Subordinates willing to work in this way are order takers and "yes men" with whom it is impossible to build an outstanding company. Instead, a keen sense of the business helps a manager know its true priorities and this helps a manager to lead. He or she can ask probing questions of subordinates, questions whose answers reflect the highest-priority issues of the business. Such questions, along with more detailed follow-up questions (when needed), set high standards. Subordinates know that their boss is well informed and concerned, and that he or she has distilled the myriad issues facing a company and focused on critical issues that will get sustained attention. By relying on questions rather than instructions, a manager can also assess the thinking and judgment of others. Of course, there are times when a manager must intervene directly and tell subordinates what to do. However, such actions can undercut their autonomy, risk taking, and sense of accomplishment. Hence, it is critical to limit top-down interventions to situations that demand it.

Personal Tools

Besides asking probing questions on critical issues, managers have several other tools to keep substantive issues dominant.

Small Groups.   First, managers can try to do as much as possible of their work with subordinates in very small groups—even one on one. Several of the executives we interviewed said that large groups were excellent devices for disseminating information but poor forums for devising new approaches to strategic or operating questions. If anything, there is usually an inverse relationship between the number of participants in a meeting and the likelihood of substantive progress on a problem. Formality increases as meetings grow larger. People become more cautious, less candid. They are sensitive to the wide variety of stakes present in the room and are reluctant to offend through criticism. With a "you scratch my back and I'll scratch yours" attitude, there is often an implicit understanding that criticism is to be restrained in front of the boss for mutual benefit. Also, people are sensitive to consuming other people's time. Often the common objective is to end the meeting, not prolong it, and contentious issues are bound to prolong it.

Clear Reasons.   Managers must be able to clearly justify the reasons for their decisions in terms of the values and economics of the company. Their explanations must be clear, direct, and persuasive. Even the best-managed companies have skeptical or cynical employees who believe that hidden agendas lurk behind official explanations. Explanations couched in general, implausible terms simply feed this destructive attitude. Moreover, most people with common sense and a little experience can see through official reasons that are actually rationalizations for compromises, political maneuvering, or failure to confront hard decisions. Managers who rely on rationalization and generalization usually underestimate the people who work for them. When they can fool their employees or colleagues with incomplete or inaccurate explanations, they should pause to consider the caliber of these people. They should also consider how failing to bamboozle others will affect their own credibility and the trust others place in them.

Keeping Others Focused on Substance

There are, of course, limits to the power of personal example, so a manager must also rely on organizational tools to keep others focused on the substance of their jobs, rather than on politics, mechanics, or ritual. How a manager uses these tools depends on the particulars of the company's market position, personnel, and values. But an underlying prejudice toward substance suggests several broad guidelines.

Reluctance to Reorganize.   The first guideline is that managers should be reluctant to pursue massive restructurings. A well-managed company is almost always changing in small ways, adding to or sometimes creating new units. However, major changes in organization can make process a dominant concern of managers and subordinates for months, or even years. New jobs, new reporting relationships, new measures and rewards all require new formal systems and informal relationships. Reorganizations reallocate power and leave new areas up for grabs. Both factors can lead employees to jockey for influence in the new order. They often compel senior managers to spend even more time adjusting the new systems for the inevitable, unanticipated problems and adjudicating the inescapable conflicts over the new responsibilities and territories within the company. Of course, some change is inevitable: major changes in strategy usually require important changes in organization. But a new organization opens a Pandora's box of urgent process issues.

    Clear Responsibilities.   The second guideline is that, to the greatest degree practical, goals and responsibilities should be clear, and these responsibilities should be assigned to specific people. The conventional wisdom about contemporary organizations is that, because their external environments are complicated and changeable, they must be inevitably complex and replete with interdependencies. Managing on this assumption is a self-fulfilling prophecy: companies will grow even more complicated. A familiar pattern is overlaying planning organizations upon operating organizations, and then— because these become so cumbersome—further overlaying "temporary" task forces. When conflicts inevitably arise, high-level committees representing affected parties are created. And when all else fails, managers can revert to matrix organizations. The problems grow worse when middle managers see management by committee at the top and mirror this in their own areas of responsibility. When everyone is responsible for something, no one is really responsible.

    Keeping Formal Systems and Structures Simple.   In response to increasing complexity, companies are evolving from hierarchies into networks. Lateral relationships with peer specialists are now a complicated overlay on the traditional, hierarchical relationship with powerful bosses. Alexander d'Arbeloff went so far as to say: "I think emphasizing hierarchy is a bad thing in an organization driven by information." He responded to this with a radical antidote, refusing to sanction the preparation of a formal organization chart.

The other executives we interviewed took less dramatic steps in the same direction. Whenever possible, they tried to simplify their organizations by eliminating layers. They also gave specific people responsibility for both developing plans for key tasks and for implementing their plans. Walter Wriston recounted advice from Peter Drucker, the elemental truth of which he said continually haunted him on his way home from work: Drucker asserted that he had never seen an organization that would not be more effective with one fewer layer of management.

At Johnson & Johnson the strategic plans of their over 150 businesses that are presented to the CEO and the corporate executive committee each consist only of a two-page statement of mission and strategy and only four numbers: unit sales volume, sales revenue, estimated net income, and estimated return on investment for two years (five years and ten years out). This document is a distillation of the results of a comprehensive plan review, often lasting three days, with the business's management and the members of the executive committee responsible for the business. The condensed plan is the basis for frank and challenging discussions between the executive committee and the company presidents. J&J management believes that the simplicity of the system keeps the focus on key issues and allows for creativity. David Clare, J&J's president, describes the process:

> The sales and profit forecasts are always optimistic in the five- and ten-year plans, but this is O.K. We want people to stretch their imaginations and think expansively. In these plans we don't anticipate failure; they are a device to open up thinking. There is no penalty for inaccuracies.
>
> If a manager insists on a course of action and we (the Executive Committee) have misgivings, nine out of ten times we will let him go ahead.
>
> Johnson & Johnson is extremely decentralized,

but that does not mean that managers are free from challenge as to what they are doing. In the final analysis, managing conflict is what management is all about. Healthy conflict is about what is right, not who is right.[5]

Line versus Staff. The executives we interviewed believed that leaner organizations and greater autonomy give action-oriented managers the chance to take responsibility. Fewer layers mean that these managers are less encumbered in carrying out their tasks and that their efforts and results are more clearly visible to senior management. The managers who perform well can then be promoted, which reinforces results-oriented values throughout the company.

The effort to assign clear responsibility is far more difficult in a staff-heavy company. Generally, because they do not want to cede authority over their businesses, managers of business units resist cooperating with corporate staffs. Business unit and product managers argue that they are closer to customers, markets, and competitors and should therefore have the dominant influence over strategic and operating decisions. They also argue that the review of their strategies by functional corporate staff members results in disjointed, parochial evaluations that often neglect the integrated "big picture" view that is essential to the development of effective strategies.

Corporate staff argue in response that they offer a more detached, objective, and sometimes more rigorous assessment of the position and opportunities of a business unit. They can also conduct analyses that cut across businesses, thus identifying opportunities for cost savings or joint efforts that a manager with a parochial business-unit perspective would not see. Planning and financial staffs can also compare the prospects for different businesses and products and make more comprehensive recommendations about the relative merits of particular proposals.

Decisions about the roles of line and staff also involve choices about the kind of corporate staff a company will build. At one end of the spectrum is a purely financial staff that gathers and compares financial data from business units and functional divisions. This staff's role is to act primarily as a scorekeeper and consolidator of information. At the other end of the spectrum are powerful functional staffs with the expertise and authority to intervene in marketing, manufacturing, product development, and other operating decisions. These staffs extend senior corporate managers' ability to oversee the numerous functional decisions that underlie the company's product/market strategies.

The contribution of good staff work is immediate and clear. Decisions can be based on better data and expert advice. But the costs of staff can be hidden and quite high. First, corporate staff become another layer separating operating managers from executives. Division managers often create their own staffs to work with corporate staff, which adds yet another layer. Second, the greater the power of the staff, the less the authority, responsibility, and quite often, the initiative of the operating managers. Third, growth in staff is usually accompanied by growth in SOPs and required procedures for approval of decisions. More and more elaborate systems create more layers and filters of information. This can create greater fear of breaking the rules and making mistakes. And it can result in an environment in which criticism—even cynicism—is the norm rather than praise. Consequently, communication can become less open. Line management can become less willing to put forth innovative ideas, whose uncertainty makes them readily subject to criticism and second guessing. Techniques, systems, and measurements can grow so cumbersome and bureaucratic that substantive issues take a back seat. The result can be a significant increase in corporate bureaucracy and a corresponding decline in innovation.

Elaborate systems are not a prerequisite for autonomy. In fact, they can undermine real autonomy because they are a vehicle for increased bureaucracy that can sap authority and initiative from subordinates. Hence, a prejudice toward substance ultimately implies that leaders should limit the number and influence of staff and give line managers, rather than staff managers, responsibilities such as planning. Of course, leaders have the responsibility to fill the vacuum left by fewer staff. They must directly probe subordinates' assessments of the competitive environment facing their units, share in the formulation of strategic objectives, and monitor and hold others accountable for progress in achieving critical objectives.

Elimination of Marginal Efforts.   Another avenue to a simpler organization is the practice of dropping marginal efforts. At its simplest level, this means eliminating marginal meetings, marginal reports, and marginal activities—any effort that does not contribute to the company's strategy and basic values. By the same token, marginal staff members must be dropped, and the role of the remainder limited. As mentioned before, the elements of organizational process—meetings, reports, and so on—tend to grow in size and power with a glacial inevitability unless managers actively resist them.

Managers must extend their campaigns against marginal activities to marginal products and businesses. A strategy of growth through acquisition or new product development often leaves executives with a range of products and businesses that outrun their abilities to manage them, even if they employ the full range of professional techniques developed for diversified companies. The symptoms of overextension include strains on cash and working capital, long periods of growth without profits, doubts expressed—often implicitly—about the company's capability and focus, and chronically overburdened and tired managers. When these symptoms appear, the pace and magnitude of a company's diversification may have been too great.

SUBSTANCE AND INTEGRITY

Even the most vigorous personal effort and careful organizational planning will not create a pure, apolitical business in which substance always triumphs over process. Indeed, the most vexing questions managers face involve commitments under uncertainty with high stakes—economic, personal, and political—on all sides. For major decisions such as these, there are ultimately no prescriptions—beyond careful reflection, good judgment, and experience—and a powerful inclination to keep an intense spotlight on substance while fighting back the constant, weedlike growth of bureaucratic process that threatens companies large and small. Before developing more elaborate formal systems, a leader must continually ask, "What is the purpose of the process?" If the answer is "to create a more professional organization" rather than "to improve people's abilities to deal with the substantive issues of strategy and operations," the leader should hesitate in adopting the new formal processes. Simplicity in structure and systems is a virtue.

When process triumphs over substance, a manager's quest for integrity becomes far more difficult. An organization's fundamental aims and shared values become weak and fuzzy as they pass through layers of organizational filters. High-caliber talent shuns bureaucracies. It is almost impossible to create a meritocracy unless objectives and responsibility are clearly defined: otherwise, when everyone is somewhat responsible for everything, it is difficult to know where credit and blame should fall. And, when people in a company communicate with each other through memos, reports, forms, ritualized meetings, and signals, then direct, candid, blunt discussions of difficult issues become rare. For the same reasons, a leader's own personal values—high ethical standards, positive faith in others, and a compelling vision of where to lead a business—become diluted, refracted, and enfeebled.

This is why the day-by-day pursuit of leadership and integrity must be guided by the prejudice advocated in this chapter. A leader's personal example must make plain to all that substance is foremost. Yet process does matter. So leaders must use the formal mechanisms and informal practices of their companies to get others to concentrate on the substance of their work, that is, on efforts that directly reinforce a company's strategy and basic values.

NOTES

1. Daniel J. Isenberg, "How Senior Managers Think," *Harvard Business Review*, November–December 1984, pp. 82–83.
2. From a draft of Chapter 1 of a forthcoming book by Abraham Zaleznik, *The Managerial Mystique: Changing Realities of Business Leadership.*
3. Jack Welch in a presentation to a Harvard Business School class, 27 April 1981.
4. For a good example of this read of John Sculley's near disastrous switch from Pepsico, Inc., to Apple Computer in John Sculley, *Odyssey* (New York: Harper & Row, 1987).
5. Robert L. Simons, "Codman & Shurtleff, Inc.—Planning and Control Systems," 187-081. Boston: Harvard Business School, 1987, pp. 8–9.

Chapter 7

CONFRONTATION VERSUS COMPROMISE

The fourth dilemma arises whenever a manager anticipates a conflict with or among others in a company and must decide whether to handle it through confrontation or compromise. The conflict can be over basic strategic goals, allocation of resources, changes in organizational systems and structures, tactical decisions, or minor issues. Conflicts can arise from differences in business judgment, from clashes between the interests of different functional areas, or from differences in values.

Consider the following situation. A forty-eight-year-old executive had just taken over as president of a medium-sized manufacturer of customized packaging materials. Profits had fallen during the last year, but the company's overall position was sound. The new executive faced several problems. One of them was, in his words: "I found a lot of weak managers and a lot of others who were very resistant to me, who just gave me lip service." This took several forms: "One was hostility, sometimes they answered questions in a very nonchalant way, and just gave me pieces of information, or at other times they would say we certainly agree with what you want to do and nothing would happen." There was also a union organizing effort in a major plant. The plant's managers had been working with a local attorney to fight the union, but the new president thought they were taking the wrong approach. Finally, he inherited a $2-million capital spending plan that included several questionable projects.

For each of these problems, the president had two broad choices. One was to confront the issue at hand directly and unearth the factors creating the conflict. The other was to move more carefully and seek ways to reduce the conflicts—

by framing issues in ways that did not agitate others, by diverting attention from highly charged topics, and by working with others to find compromises that would leave all the parties reasonably satisfied with the outcomes.

At first glance, this seems like a simple problem, perhaps a "no-brainer." It is easy to sit in a chair, far removed from this situation, and conclude that the president of the company should have taken direct action and confronted the issues facing him. And, in fact, the president had taken the job with a sense of confidence and determination. He had already run, quite successfully, a major division of a *Fortune* 500 company. He said his new job "was basically an opportunity to be the true CEO of a publicly held company and a real challenge to see what kind of ability I had." Yet, once he started work and found himself immersed in the situation, he suffered through what he called "the high point of anxiety in my life."

To understand his reaction, think about the many situations most managers have faced in which, in principle, they should have confronted a difficult issue head-on but decided not to do so. In some cases, the explanation is simply a lack of courage. But more often there are deeper, more complex reasons.

The political philosophy of leadership explains these reasons clearly and persuasively. It advocates judicious compromise and recommends confrontation only as a last resort. Confrontation and conflict often create destructive by-products. In the situation above, for example, reducing or altering the capital spending plans would create skeptical winners and resentful, perhaps hostile losers who would be quite unhappy with their new leader. Some of the winners—whose projects survived—could be aggravated that an outsider had interfered with plans that they and their long-time colleagues had thought about and settled upon. With distance from a situation, it is easy to say "business is business," and conclude that the president obviously should have altered the spending plans; but relationships within the executive team could be poisoned for years to come. Similarly, if the new president intervened in the union organizing drive—by taking over the effort himself or getting another outside consultant—resentment was likely among the managers who had devised the current approach and had begun to implement it. Their credibility with their own subordinates was also at risk. The new president was already having problems, as indicated by the "lip service." This could have grown worse down the road. Moreover, the company could not afford to lose several of the resisting managers because they had had close relationships with major customers.

In the long run, the new president would need the enthusiastic support of these managers. They would implement whatever capital spending plans the company agreed upon, and some of them would be directly responsible for the hands-on, detailed effort to avoid a union. If they resented their new leader, both efforts would suffer. The new president had to face the possibility that the managers who disagreed with him were right. He did not know them well and was new to their business. If he confronted them directly, he could be proven wrong. This would sap what little credibility and trust he had. As the political philosophy stresses, there is rarely a single "right" answer to the complex issues managers face. Compromise is often the right way to reconcile conflicting but, nevertheless, important factors.

In addition, direct confrontation violated the style and culture of the company. It had operated successfully for decades on the "good old boy" system. The same managers, who knew and trusted each other, had resolved difficulties without direct, open confrontations. Confronting these issues directly was thus very risky: it meant doing battle against the established and successful culture of the company.

Both the *directive* and the *values-driven* perspectives reject this reasoning. They share the fear that compromise or even the appearance of it will breed more politics and reinforce the status quo. If political maneuvering, resistance, or lip service change a company's decisions, people will know it, and so maneuver and resist harder the next time. This squanders resources, frustrates a manager's efforts to accomplish objectives, and biases information throughout a company.

Both philosophies assert that confrontation can be constructive and improve decision making. But this occurs only when problems are clearly identified and put on the table for all to see. People respond to direct challenges, so confronting issues can increase the vigor with which facts are pursued and alternatives evaluated. Moreover, it can be a powerful antidote to politicization, diverting attention from self-interest and increasing the openness of decision making. According to these philosophies, decisions are more focused and fewer resources are squandered on the side payments needed for compromise. In fact, directive leaders sometimes welcome conflict because it generates new ideas and disrupts the status quo.

Compromise tends to shift attention to the *process* of negotiation. Confrontation can ensure that the search for the facts on which decisions are based is more thorough; it can also ensure that the debate about alternative plans of action is more complete and objective. Confrontation on important issues can clarify and reinforce the company's goals, whereas compromise can create ambiguity and uncertainty. When corporate goals and standards become clearer, localitis diminishes. In addition, a company can concentrate its resources on activities that build competitive strength rather than satisfy internal constituencies. In contrast, compromise usually means departing from a strategically optimal course.

From this perspective, the new president was playing for very high stakes. He needed to know in detail the rationale for the current capital spending program and for the current effort to resist the union, because he would have to live with the results of both: higher wages and work rules at a major plant, and depletion or waste of the company's limited funds. Further, the lip service was a direct attack on his authority. From the viewpoint of directive leadership, he should not tolerate it. Finally, the company's established values may have needed a change. Perhaps the old boy system was too cozy and close-minded. This could even explain why the company's performance had been adequate but not better.

THE PREJUDICE

To understand the right prejudice for the dilemma of confrontation versus compromise, consider what the new president actually did. First, he met at length with everyone involved in the effort to discourage employees from joining a union. He asked why they had adopted the approach they had, and he questioned them in detail about their thinking. He explained why he thought it made more sense to take a different approach, and he recommended that they choose a new outside adviser. He left the final decision up to them—and they ultimately chose to change their approach. He also halted all but the most essential of the $2-million capital spending plan he inherited. Additional spending was approved only after he and his managers had worked closely together in scores of meetings at which they analyzed and debated the prospects for their products and businesses. He explained that the company's falling profits made it necessary to be much more careful about spending, that he needed to understand the new projects in detail, and that everyone would get a full, fair hearing before he or the company's top executives decided anything.

He described his approach to the managers who were skeptical about him or who resisted his early efforts in the following way:

I gradually began putting people in some basic categories. This was very, very subjective but I had little else to go on. One group was people I thought had some potential and who could be persuaded to get on board with what I wanted to do. I met with them for lunch, for dinner, and in a lot of meetings and tried to make clear to them the direction in which I wanted to move.

With the ones who were hostile, I said bluntly: "You aren't supporting us. What is the problem?" I also said: "Decide whether you want to be on this team or off it." I told them I was leveling with them and expected them to level with me. I said I would be as reasonable as

I could and that everyone would get a chance to become more comfortable with me and with the new approach we would take.

Careful examination of the approach the new president took reveals a great deal.

Above all, it implies a clear prejudice: that is, when situations pull managers back and forth between compromise and confrontation, their bias should be toward confrontation.

In his award-winning book *Leadership*, James MacGregor Burns has observed that the willingness to confront conflict characterizes leaders. He writes, "Leaders, whatever their professions of harmony, do not shun conflict; they confront it, exploit it, ultimately embody it."[1] They view conflict, not only as a means to better, more thoughtful decisions, but as a stimulus to change and a constant challenge to the inertial forces within organizations that spawn bureaucracy and reinforce the status quo. General George Patton once observed, "No one was thinking when everyone was thinking the same thing." But a simple prejudice toward confrontation is very general, and situations involving intense, potentially divisive conflicts must be handled with great care, so it is critical to understand precisely what this prejudice does and does not imply.

Not a Heavy-Handed Approach.   Above all, this prejudice does not imply a heavy-handed, dictatorial imposition of will. Many executives make arbitrary, unilateral decisions to avoid conflict. By giving orders, they avoid debate. Of course, this does not resolve conflict. Instead, the issue festers and people express their discomfort indirectly, often in damaging ways. A prejudice for confrontation must be tempered by a concern for people's feelings, their sense of dignity, and the importance of their sense of ownership and control over their operations. Reuben Mark summed it up this way:

If you think someone is headed nowhere, you've got to say, "I think you're headed nowhere." Now, whether you do it frontally at a meeting with others around, or whether you end the meeting and then circle around to his office that afternoon and say, "I've been doing some thinking and I think you've got some great stuff, but I think that it may make sense to go this way instead of that way," you have to end up with agreement on direction and principles. In as nice a way as possible, you have to let them know what you think.

Focus on Substance Not Personalities. Although a manager must be keenly aware of both, the focus of this prejudice is confrontation based on the substance of the issues, not the personalities or personal stakes involved. When people in an organization know that major as well as minor conflicts will be resolved frontally and on the basis of their merits—and that personal attacks are not acceptable—they will substantially reduce their tendencies toward politicizing and bureaucracy. One executive distinguished between these two approaches: "Conflict to stimulate thought and ideas is one thing. But to have it be an edict accompanied by faultfinding is something else."

Debate over Issues. The essence of this prejudice is to make explicit whatever issues are causing a conflict, and then encourage an open, unconstrained debate on their substance. This is what the new president in our example did on each of the issues facing him. The dominant question in this debate must be: What resolution of these issues makes the greatest long-term sense for the company? The leaders we interviewed were comfortable with a work environment in which debates could be vigorous, even impassioned. One said, "We have huge arguments." However, the bone of contention in these discussions should be issues, not personalities.

The leaders we talked to were less concerned about whether a debate would produce winners and losers than whether it would lead to the right decision. Richard Munro described a meeting in which he knew his executive vice president for planning and a top line executive would disagree sharply over whether the company should make a very large acquisition. He was concerned that the discussion could become a personal contest rather than an objective assessment of the two views. He described his approach in this way:

> There's always a little of, "I won that one and he lost." But the last thing you want to do is make it a personal contest. We try like hell to wring out the emotions and make the debate as dispassionate a process as we can, based on the merits of the issue. The only way it will end without a winner and a loser is if one side of the argument is genuinely more persuasive than the other. My role will be to probe both of their cases.

When confrontation is based on the facts, not on personalities, it can become somewhat less painful to "lose." In fact, losing one "big" war, based on differences in judgments about the facts, may be less painful in the long run than continually losing a lot of personal little battles. A clear decision also allows subordinates to redirect their energies more quickly to objectives and activities that can lead somewhere.

Personal Example.   The risk in encouraging open confrontations is that they will spill over into personality clashes and harsh battles over turf, driven by localitis. To avoid this, leaders need to show by their own example that open confrontation is desirable—so long as it is done in a spirit of mutual respect and goodwill. They should seek to minimize the negative side effects of conflict through their personal commitments to meritocracy, their belief in the abilities of others, and the shared values of their companies.

Many of the CEOs provided a personal example of candor and openness by having explicit "open door" policies. People who walked through their doorway could expect to get candid reactions to their ideas and questions. Furthermore, these leaders frequently left their offices to visit various parts of their companies. On these visits, they did not simply "manage by walking around." They encouraged people to ask questions, even on sensitive issues, and they responded to them as candidly as possible. Richard Munro said:

I spend an enormous amount of time encouraging openness. I speak about it every chance I get. One of the most
important things I do is to protect the very fragile environment in which that can happen. I see an enormous
number of people. My day is so filled it's unbelievable. I
have a two-hour breakfast every two weeks with twenty-
five randomly selected employees. It lasts two hours. It's
off the record—anything goes. We talk about their problems. I tell them where I think the company is going. I
try to make it a real, honest-to-God dialogue. We work
and work and work on this, and I don't give up.

Executives set a personal example by the way they
discuss important issues with each other. Alexander d'Arbeloff commented: "Open exchange is part of the culture. I'm
open and the other founder was open. There were a lot of
arguments between us. We set the example."

James Burke explained the importance of openness
and conflict in overcoming a politicized environment at Johnson & Johnson:

The basic change [the COO] and I have brought to this
company has been openness. I think the organization is
less politicized, makes better decisions, and is a happier
place to work the more open you can make it. On balance, I have a conviction that it is a lot easier to let it all
hang out—to be blunt. The cost is that at times I hurt
people when I don't intend to.

When I first came to this company, it was not
open at all. It was highly political. I was here a year and
then I quit. . . . I couldn't stand it. We were losing market share in all but 8 percent of our consumer businesses. Everybody was writing "cover your ass" memos.
Whenever you got in an argument, people were pulling
things from the file. When I came back, I was determined
to fix this. I came out of a company [P&G] that was a
very successful environment, very honest, and not very

political. It was based on who was going to produce. It was honest and objective in its appraisal—sometimes, I thought, too much so.

I have a rule that I want to be able to go to anyone, anywhere in the organization, and get anything I want. The day that I don't, the person that deprives me of it is gone. I tell my people. "You can't have it both ways. You've wanted us to be open with you, and we have been. Now let's see whether you can do it with your own organization."

At times, the leaders we interviewed said or did things that gave the appearance of compromise. They compromised on some issues, they sometimes pulled their punches in criticizing others' ideas, and they sometimes tabled controversial issues for consideration later. In these cases, however, they tempered their criticisms, not because of politically motivated opportunism, but because they were aware of the power of their positions and had a sense of respect and compassion for the people with whom they worked. Moreover, pulling a punch did not mean the leader would not communicate his thinking—clearly—on a later occasion. When issues they considered critical were at stake, such as the values, long-term direction, and underlying economics of their companies, they stood firm.

Sensitivity to Timing.   A prejudice for confrontation requires a leader be sensitive to timing and to the merits of patience in certain situations. When executives we interviewed tabled controversial issues, it was usually not to avoid conflict. Rather, they followed the maxim, "You don't have to shoot the tiger the first time out."

Moreover, to encourage open debate, they sometimes waited to disclose their own views. This is not because they were maneuvering opportunistically or holding their cards close to their vests. Often they wanted to stimulate further debate among others and thereby improve the quality of the ultimate decision. They were concerned that people would interpret a question or statement from the "boss" as the final word on a subject. (This still happened despite their best attempts.) Walter Wriston explained his thoughts this way:

> I don't think you compromise on the economics side.
> You jump in when your sense tells you that the enterprise is in some jeopardy or that there is a human being
> down there that is screwing it up for the people around
> him. But when I know others disagree with what I think
> is the best course of action, I often don't express my
> opinion. I could be wrong. If there are very good people
> that are much divided, it is clear we ought to think about
> it a little bit more. Stating my opinion could freeze the
> debate.

Some of this behavior could appear compromising and maneuvering to an outside observer. The risk that this will happen is lower if managers have already spent a great deal of time and effort directly confronting tough issues and conflicts and consistently encourage others to do the same. Although leaders need not confront all important issues themselves, they must work hard to create an environment in which others feel free to debate an issue's facts and assumptions. In addition, they must be skilled at asking probing questions that keep issues in focus and the stakes and standards for performance high.

Compromise, Consensus, and Pseudo-Agreement

The rationale for a prejudice toward confronting conflict rests on another consideration: the secondary, often unintended consequences of compromise. Compromises often fail to achieve their principal objectives—avoiding the creation of winners and losers and fostering cooperation. Unless people are either absolutely convinced of another point of view or see that a new way will work and agree to it, they often harbor doubts about the compromise agreement. Under these circumstances, as they work underground for ways to press their own points of view, their cooperation remains superficial.

Frequent negotiation also undermines a manager's authority and power. As one concession leads to another, compromise can become a slippery slope. Strategy then reflects internal political stakes rather than external competitive realities. Creating a pattern of compromise, a manager appears reactive. The initiative then rests with the others involved with the issues on which conflict arises and who can influence outcomes by polarizing a debate.

The popular prescription—seeking compromise to achieve consensus around critical decisions—is seriously flawed. Certainly, consensus is better than fragmented support of a planned action. But on issues where opinions diverge widely and where stakes are high, does compromise create true consensus? Or does it create only a charade?

When compromise masquerades as consensus, decisions suffer. Followers do not know what their leader's real concerns and thinking are, and the issues causing the serious conflicts continue to fester only to reappear in other situations.

Compromise begets more compromise and raises the risk that people will start to bargain away a company's basic values and norms. In a corporate setting, those values are often very fragile. If they are to be a real force in a company, they cannot be compromised. Repeated compromise sends an increasingly persuasive message that the management does not consider its values to be important. When basic values are compromised, a manager's personal credibility and power are also affected. Irving Shapiro observed:

> Don't compromise at all. Once the organization knows you can be sweet-talked, you're dead for practical purposes. The organization has to accept the premise that you're going to call the shots on the basic, fundamental issues of running the business.

It is a mistake to think that negotiation and compromise nurture consensus. Those who believe this fail to distinguish the effects of compromise *in a particular situation* and its effects *over time*. A clear pattern of negotiation and compromise undermines genuine consensus. Commitment to shared goals and values is the fundamental source of consensus in an organization. A readiness to negotiate and compromise sends repeated signals to members that the underlying goals are also subject to negotiation. When this occurs, people perceive that top management is not fully committed to those goals.

As a result, the power of shared goals to mold consensus deteriorates substantially. People tend to support decisions that they believe are made fairly, with the intention of serving a common purpose, and based on the decision makers' well-informed judgment, after a careful weighing of the different positions and with respect for the individuals involved. Such an approach can even help proponents of a losing viewpoint find it easier to commit to a course of action. Even though they may have argued against the decision, they at least have had their "day in court," and in a court perceived as fair.

Confrontation and Integrity

The quest for integrity in the face of management dilemmas leads to a prejudice for confronting rather than shunning conflict. Among the personal values central to integrity are honesty and fairness. Masking one's views or denying them is hardly honest. Nor is it fair to let others make judgments and decisions on the basis of misleading assumptions. Also, because leaders are strongly committed to their visions and plans for their companies, they are reluctant to compromise them to avoid confrontations with others. The pursuit of integrity also involves working toward certain organizational aims and norms, among them trust, mutual respect, and vigorous debate about problems. When managers confront issues and the people who disagree with them and when they expect others to do the same, they demonstrate that they respect the abilities and judgments of others and trust them to treat issues fairly and honestly. They are also showing by example how much they value open communication. A bias toward fair, direct, respectful confrontation, based on the substance of issues, can permeate an organization, positively influencing other managers' decisions.

NOTE

1. James MacGregor Burns, *Leadership* (New York: Harper & Row, 1978), p. 39.

Chapter 8

TANGIBLES VERSUS INTANGIBLES

The last dilemma arising from the tensions among the three philosophies of leadership is the conflict between tangible and intangible considerations. Consider these situations.

In 1963, a talented senior executive of a Dallas-based oil company wrote an article in a popular national magazine. The article strongly criticized the Dallas community, particularly the "establishment," for its reaction to President Kennedy's assassination. The article appeared under the author's name, but it did not identify his company. Nevertheless, the article created a furor in the Dallas area directed not only at the executive but also at his company. Some customers and suppliers threatened to take their business elsewhere. Shortly thereafter, because of pressure from his superiors, the executive left his company. Did they handle the situation in the right way?

A very large, well-known U.S. company had been run for decades on its founder's vision that the company should consist of small, decentralized operating units headed by managers who were genuinely in charge of their businesses. The company had succeeded in making this vision real, and its division managers were proud of running their own shows. They believed, as did many outside observers, that much of the company's success resulted from the innovation and marketing responsiveness that the commitment to bottom-up decision making and autonomy fostered.

Then, a large, very centralized competitor began taking business away. It offered the same range of products, placed computer terminals in the offices of its customers' purchasing agents, had only one salesperson calling on the customers and representing the entire product line, and offered discounts to customers who bought the full range of its products. To respond to this competitor, the company would have to consolidate the sales and service efforts of its autonomous divisions, coordinate their pricing, centralize inventory control and logistics, and—ultimately, perhaps—coordinate the new product development efforts of its divisions. When the company's chief executive raised this issue with his division heads, he heard vigorous, negative reactions to the moves toward centralization. Implicit in several of these objections was the threat that some of his best division presidents would look for jobs elsewhere. What considerations should have dominated the CEO's decisions in this situation?

A manager was responsible for making and marketing a new pesticide in a developing country. The pesticide promised to be a spectacular success and make a large contribution to the country's agricultural development. The parent company badly needed such a success. Moreover, the manager's career would benefit greatly if the product succeeded. Things were going well when the manager received a toxicologist's report that preliminary studies of laboratory animals suggested that the pesticide could cause health problems for farm workers. An investigation into this possibility could take up to two years, which would cut returns on the investment and allow time for competitors to introduce similar products. The country in which the manager was working had no laws or regulations requiring him to take any further action in response to the toxicologist's report. What should he have done?

All three of these cases involve a conflict between tangibles and intangibles—the ever-present tension between immediate pressures and opportunities and the less certain, less tangible, and often subtle considerations lying in the distant future. Pressing, tangible pressures often involve dimensions of performance that are readily quantifiable and measurable, such as current profitability, growth, or productivity. They can also involve localitis, pursuit of self-interest, bonuses, promotions, prestige, and so on. All of these are far less ambiguous than complex strategic issues, personal values, company values, social obligations, and a leader's vision for a company—subtle and intangible considerations vital to integrity and leadership.

Among the conflicts between tangibles and intangibles, four are very common for managers.

Short-Term Factors versus Long-Term Factors. This is the widely recognized and much discussed tension between short-term factors, such as curtailing of R&D, postponing of plant expansions, employee cutbacks, shortcuts in quality, and other cost-cutting efforts, which raise near-term profits; and long-term efforts, such as the development of new products, major improvements to manufacturing processes, enhancing a product's value through better quality or technical features, and entry into new markets or businesses, whose benefits are more distant and less certain. In many of its forms, this is essentially a conflict between current and long-term financial performance.

Ethical Standards versus Corporate Performance. The second common conflict occurs when a manager's own personal values clash with actions likely to improve his or her company's financial performance, and often the manager's own compensation. The Dallas oil executive who wrote the controversial article faced a conflict between his personal ethical values and the company's performance that challenged management in two separate ways. First of all, top management had to consider whether the executive should have written the article at all. He should have known that the probability of a backlash from customers was high. The financial consequences for the company were likely to be immediate, direct, and significant. Yet, the executive had strong convictions about the issue, and his conscience told him he had an obligation to speak out. The second level of the problem confronted the president of the company, after the article had been published. He had to decide what to do. Should he punish the man who wrote the article to placate customers and suppliers and ensure their continued business? Or should he sacrifice company performance in the interest of intangible considerations, in this case his own personal belief in freedom of speech and adherence to one's own conscience and personal values? The president found himself in a situation not unlike the executive who had written the article.

Corporate Values versus Competitive Pressures. A third common conflict occurs when a company's basic values clash with immediate competitive pressures. The CEO in the large, decentralized company with a strong faith in autonomous divisions faced this conflict when the company confronted a highly centralized, efficient adversary. On the one hand, the abiding values of local autonomy and a sense of ownership at the division level had served the company well for decades. But on the other hand, it was clear that duplication of efforts and higher costs were letting a very powerful competitor make inroads into the company's markets, causing immediate financial damage.

Company Social Obligations versus Financial Performance. For the chemical company manager faced with the toxicologist's report, both the immediate, measurable benefits for the company and his career considerations argued strongly for proceeding according to schedule with the pesticide. The concerns on the other side of the scale were far less clear: the responsibility of the company to workers who might be harmed by its product and, perhaps, a responsibility to assess potential hazards thoroughly, even when the laws of the country in which the product would be used did not require such procedures. The decision was made even more difficult by other intangibles: on the one hand, the benefits of more rapid agricultural development in the country, and on the other, the damage to the self-respect of the manager should he knowingly risk the health of farm workers in the cause of his career.

THE PERSPECTIVES OF THE THREE PHILOSOPHIES

Each leadership philosophy suggests a very different way of thinking about any of the common conflicts among tangibles and intangibles. Managers inclined toward either the directive or values-driven approaches will believe that their personal values and strategic visions should dominate their decisions, that their values and strategies should be unambiguously clear, and that these should not be compromised. For directive leadership, this orientation raises the prospect of conflict with the interests, values, or ethical standards of others in the company. In the case of the oil executive, for instance, his personal values clashed with those of his superiors. They assessed the situation and his behavior differently, and ultimately he had to resign.

Values-driven leadership presupposes that a leader's personal values are in harmony with the values of a company. Hence, even in the face of internal political pressures, leaders are reluctant to compromise these intangibles. Because they are unwilling to compromise, they too are more likely to face conflict in order to preserve what they value.

Managers inclined toward the political philosophy tend to make no presumptions about whose values, or standards, should dominate in a particular situation. They forge a strategy by responding to others' ideas and initiatives, whatever they are. Such leaders are much more inclined to remain emotionally detached from a situation and to try to maintain their flexibility from situation to situation. When there are conflicting organizational interests, some involving tangibles and others involving intangibles, political-minded leaders will be more inclined to seek a compromise that satisfies the parties involved.

THE DILEMMA'S INTRICACIES

Conflicts between tangible and intangible concerns are extremely difficult to resolve, for reasons that go well beyond the differences among the three philosophies of leadership.

The Muddle of Intangibles

First, it is not possible to translate all competing considerations and responsibilities into a single common denominator, such as dollars and cents. Of course, company values and personal ethical standards do have financial and competitive consequences. But some of these—relating to values, standards, and broad strategic visions—have consequences that are indirect and very subtle. They often defy quantification.

For example, in the case of the company that had for decades prized decentralization, how can one quantify the current and future value of the additional effort and creativity unleashed when middle managers and division heads genuinely believe they are responsible for their operations? In the case of the chemical company, there is no way that the manager can calculate the risks of a possible health hazard without running a two-year toxicological study. In addition, the study could prove to be inaccurate, and the full consequences might not be known until years after the product had been introduced and used. Moreover, no one can place a quantitative or dollars and cents value on irresponsible behavior. One could, of course, speculate on how, sometime later, the host country might punish the company for selling a dangerous product. Also, someone could estimate the financial benefit to the country of improving its agricultural yield. But how does one measure the costs to a company or to a manager that arise from the simple fact that it may have done something that is socially irresponsible and violated the consciences of some of its members? Without knowing these costs, it is impossible to weigh them against whatever benefits may arise from going ahead and marketing the pesticide.

A simple approach, in either case, would be to dismiss the frustratingly intangible considerations. But this supposes that what matters for managers is only what accountants can measure.

The second difficulty of weighing tangibles against intangibles is that the chain of cause and effect linking company values, ethical standards, and strategic vision with performance is extremely complicated and often obscure. Actions that are dubious or unethical may, at first glance, have no consequences beyond their immediate situations. But a leader's behavior sets an example for others in the company. It can reinforce norms and values or undercut them. In any case, however, the effects of a leader's example will ripple outward in subtle, sometimes invisible ways. Today's example at the top will not directly or clearly determine tomorrow's behavior at the middle levels of a company. But, even though it cannot be predicted or calibrated, its influence is there.

Perhaps the most vexing of all conflicts are those involving personal ethical standards. Here the intangibles are matters of basic personal beliefs and values. These differ from person to person, and persuasion or examination of the facts often cannot reconcile them. They usually involve judgments about gray areas in which facts and ethical standards are unclear. Moreover, because managers often have little practice thinking rigorously about the ethical aspects of their work, issues involving personal values can easily become emotionally charged, further hampering constructive communication. After the national magazine published the article by the Dallas oil executive, tempers flared within the management ranks of his company and scores of people sent critical letters or complained by phone. Some condemned the article, while others vigorously defended it. Heat, not light, dominated the situation.

The Tyranny of the Tangible

The final factor that makes the conflict between tangibles and intangibles so difficult is the "tyranny of the tangible." The struggle between tangibles and intangibles is not a fair fight. Powerful forces push organizations to sacrifice long-term, intangible considerations for short-term tangibles. The tangible draws power from many sources, of which three are very common.

Foremost among the sources of this tyranny are the individual and group interests that the political philosophy of leadership describes as localitis. Consider, for example, the position of the division managers in the highly decentralized company facing an efficient, centralized adversary. By resisting centralization in their own organizations, each division manager was defending his or her own turf. None of them wanted to cede the authority, responsibility, and the rewards of being in charge of a division. No doubt, in some of these cases, self-interest and narrow-mindedness were at work. But many of the division executives truly believed that the decentralized philosophy was the best way to run the entire company. They knew this from their own experience and believed decades of successful performance confirmed their view. In this situation, the strategic risk, somewhere down the road, did not weigh as heavily with the division managers as did the immediate, local concerns.

A second reason that tangibles tend to dominate intangibles is that people generally fear uncertainty and try to avoid it. But uncertainty pervades most strategic issues. They involve judgments about the future, about which there are very few facts. Strategic choices also involve executives' personal values, another set of subtle, intangible factors. And strategic decisions involve outcomes with medium- and long-term horizons, which further compound uncertainties. Instead of wrestling with these problems of uncertainty, many people find it more satisfying to work on immediate, solvable, operating problems. They convince themselves that their task is to do what lies clearly at hand, not to worry about possibilities in a distant, unknowable future. Even senior executives, who should have their eyes focused on the future often flee from strategic uncertainties into "fire-fighting," the familiar preoccupation with today's tangibles.

A third factor that reinforces the power of tangibles is a widespread ideology among U.S. companies. It tells executives how to keep score in the game of competition. The critical measures are return on investment, quarterly earnings, and stock prices. To succeed in this contest, broad financial targets must be translated into budgets, standards, and ratios that usually take the form of short-term, quantifiable benchmarks. In companies where this ideology has taken hold, systems and structures reinforce the importance of measurable, near-term financial performance. The result? Concerns for immediate profitability readily divert attention from less measurable strategic issues. Because strategic goals cannot be readily quantified, they usually do not have a prominent role in compensation systems or performance criteria. Consequently, subordinates can dismiss their importance. After all, regardless of what the bosses may say about their commitment to long-term strategic goals, others see the way their bosses measure their performance and the things for which they are held accountable as the true indicators of what their bosses want.

Eventually, of course, customers, the financial markets, and the markets for management talent will punish a company that continues to ignore less tangible, longer-term considerations. But this punishment may be inflicted only after the damage is irreversible. A company's competitive position, reputation, and talent may have suffered beyond repair.

Even though the playing field on which tangibles and intangibles compete is not level, and localitis, uncertainty, and short-term pressures accentuate immediate concerns, this dilemma, nevertheless, proves very difficult to resolve. Either intuitively or from experience, many managers know that intangibles give leaders and their companies powerful advantages. This is why the philosophy of values-driven leadership is so persuasive, even though—unlike the other two philosophies—it is not so readily apparent how its precepts translate into practice. The essence of values-driven leadership is infusing intangibles into decision making throughout a company. According to this philosophy, when a company's work environment helps its managers and employees fulfill their basic human needs and values, the company can differentiate itself from its competition through more intense commitment, harder work, and better decisions, products, and services. Such an environment makes it easier for a company to attract top-caliber personnel and fully tap their potential. These people can be given greater autonomy, which helps the company respond quickly to external changes and enhances its creativity, initiative, and risk taking. As people in a company come to believe that one person can make a difference, and as they see a company as an outlet for their desires to create something of value, their work becomes more meaningful. This further increases their motivation, and may even reduce localitis in the company.

In contrast, many other ways of securing competitive advantage prove to be more transient. New technology and other innovations migrate quickly from company to company. In industries such as consumer electronics, the half-life of a product is sometimes measured in months. In financial services, complex innovations can be copied even more quickly. The markets for technology, scientific expertise, and managerial talent are worldwide. Because knowledge or know-how migrates quickly among companies, competitive advantage that has a narrow base can erode quickly.

Intangibles matter because a company's strategic vision, the values and norms that reinforce it, and the moral standards that guide its dealings with employees and outsiders, all create a community. It is vastly more difficult to copy a complex competitive social system than to reverse engineer a product. Once a social system is harnessed to an innovative strategy, a company can become a dominant competitor for years. The so-called Toyota production system—which includes commitments to ever-increasing quality and ever-diminishing costs, lifetime employment, and a sense of commitment to the company extending from the shop floor to the executive ranks—is only one example of how a social system coupled to a powerful strategy can transform an industry. In this case, Toyota has been displacing the industry's most powerful companies, General Motors and Ford, which for decades had seemed invulnerable to overseas competition. The real terms of competition turn heavily on intangibles rather than tangibles. Most managers sense this even amidst the press of their companies' immediate, daily concerns.

THE PREJUDICE

When tangible concerns such as profits, performance, budgets, or localitis conflict with intangibles such as personal ethics, a company's values and strategic vision, or its social obligations, a twofold prejudice provides critical guidance. First, managers who aspire to outstanding performance must make unswerving commitments to the highest standards of ethical behavior and personal integrity. This holds true regardless of the situation. Its rationale is clear and compelling: high ethical standards are at the core of the idea of integrity that we described in the Introduction to Part II. Without them, the deep personal aspirations and idealistic organizational aims that are central to business leadership are likely to be stillborn.

The second part of this prejudice is more complicated, and the rest of this chapter discusses it in detail. In essence, it is a powerful predisposition to seek ways, especially through personal effort and example, to ensure that intangible considerations powerfully influence a company's decision making. To fight the tyranny of the tangible, managers must work hard to make intangibles as real, immediate, vivid, and powerful as possible.

Both parts of this prejudice help protect companies from the tyranny of the tangible, as long as managers show powerful biases toward intangibles. If senior managers do not find ways to level the playing field and balance tangibles and intangibles, others in a company are unlikely to do so. Facing no resistance, localitis, self-interest, and fear of uncertainty will dominate, causing people to flee from the subtle and distant to the immediate and doable. People will cast aside intangibles such as a broad vision and other company values and norms that are vital to competitive success. Managers seeking outstanding results may work incrementally or directly, but they must *always* act with a powerful prejudice toward the intangibles that the values-driven philosophy advocates.

Making Intangibles Tangible

How can a manager make subtle and elusive intangibles real and present? The basic answer sounds simple enough: first, become aware of the intangible consequences of routine decisions; and, second, rely heavily on personal effort and example to communicate these to others.

How management and control systems are designed is one example of the first part of this answer. We have already discussed the adverse consequences of compensation systems based only on tangible, short-term, measurable criteria. Planning, budgeting, measurement, reward, and management development systems all require careful development to ensure not only that they don't divert attention from intangible concerns, but also that they concretely communicate intangible concerns. Ryoichi Kawai, the man who led Komatsu's competitive attack on Caterpillar, stressed the importance of this aspect of his company's management systems to its performance and employee development. He said:

> Tangible results from these [management] systems were twofold—increased market share through quality improvement and productivity improvement leading to cost reduction. But equally important is the achievement of the intangibles, such as improved communication among departments and setting up of clear, common goals.[1]

The responsibility for making intangibles more tangible is inescapably the responsibility of senior management. Any attempts to delegate responsibility for resisting the tyranny of the tangible are doomed. Why? At lower levels in the organization, the splintering forces of localitis, self-interest, standard operating procedures, fire fighting, and the immediate gratification of working on today's problems *all* push aside longer-term, more subtle considerations. Unfortunately, many managers more or less fail at this responsibility. They ritualistically invoke strategic vision and testify to the importance of ethical standards and company values in speeches that have the tone and persuasiveness of commencement day addresses. Once middle managers have heard these speeches two or three times, most tend to regard them as empty words, usually followed by "business as usual."

This skeptical view is widespread. It poses one of the greatest challenges to managers who want to make intangibles real and influential. The skeptical view is misleading, however. It can fool managers by implying that words or speeches or personal statements do not matter very much. That is wrong: they do matter. Several of the leaders we interviewed were quite emphatic about this. Ralph Bailey said:

> I want to make sure everybody knows what we are in business to accomplish. We are in business to make a profit by playing within the rules. The rules are that we are going to operate a company utilizing the highest business and personal ethics, and that we plan to pay close attention to our social responsibilities along the way. We intend to be the low-cost operator and will accept nothing less as a goal for ourselves. We intend to pay close attention to our people and close attention to their development, to develop our organization from within. We intend to be highly accountable. We intend to be very compassionate. It is always my intention to exercise power very carefully. We expect other managers to do the same thing. You must make your managerial philosophy known within an organization and demonstrate it by your own personal actions.

Consistent Words and Actions.   Words matter. Executives must be clear, convincing, and at times even repetitive in stating their companies' strategic visions, the values that they expect others to hold high, and the importance of high ethical standards.

Beyond this, what matters is that actions are consistent with words. Walter Wriston commented, "You have to be absolutely consistent in the pursuit of your values. Otherwise, you can forget it." But what does consistent behavior mean? Surely, it does not mean that all situations, people, and problems will be forced into the same cookie-cutter approach. That would be rigidity, not consistency. The varied demands of executive work doom rigid managers to limited careers.

What consistency means is that the same fundamental principles will be applied to the variety of problems, situations, and personalities that a manager faces. These are *principles*, not precise, rigid rules. For example, managers cannot resolve all problems raising ethical issues in exactly the same way. But they should be resolved only after a leader asks what course of action is the right one: that is, what course of action is the one with which people can live and work in good conscience. The real test of a manager's consistency is how infrequently others must guess about what kind of thinking he or she will use when approaching a vexing problem. They may not know what the final decision will be. But if their superiors are consistent, subordinates will have a sense of the values and concerns their superiors will bring to bear in making the decision. Walter Wriston put it this way: "Stand for consistency in purpose and values; guys that love you one day and beat you the next don't build any kind of organization."

Follow-Up. Even a consistent, principled approach is insufficient. Managers must do more to make elusive values and other intangibles more effective and persuasive. Follow-up is extremely important. As Alexander d'Arbeloff observed:

> If I'm going to follow up on something, everybody knows they better do it because I *am* going to follow up. You can't follow up on everything. You have to be selective. It has got to be on a very few things; they have to be important; and everyone has to know there will be follow-up.

Challenge. A close kin to follow-up is visible impatience with people whose actions are at odds with the intangibles a leader values highly. D'Arbeloff described how he dealt with people who did not share this value: "Guys have been let go because of a lack of candor, including some very able people. This business is information-driven in spades. I want everyone to be open."

Implicit in d'Arbeloff's remarks is a willingness to challenge people who seem to share neither a company's values nor a commitment to its strategic vision. Such challenges often awaken people to the importance of values and to senior executives' commitment to them. As we explained in Chapter 3, when James Burke concluded that commitment to Johnson & Johnson's credo had grown weak, he held a long series of meetings in which he asked division managers whether they accepted the credo and whether they believed it mattered. If it didn't matter, Burke felt, it should be torn off the wall and abolished.

Looking back on the exercise, Burke felt that the very act of discussing and directly challenging people about these values actually heightened their awareness of Johnson & Johnson's values and the role they played in its business. In fact, several years later, Johnson & Johnson responded to an episode of product tampering by voluntarily withdrawing all its Tylenol capsules, at a cost exceeding a hundred million dollars. Burke concluded that the company acted as quickly and as correctly as it did because of the deep commitment to the credo and to the priorities it expressed, which guided people's decisions and allowed the organization to coalesce swiftly around those decisions.

Paying a Price. The price of consistency can be high. It requires vigilance. If values or other intangibles are allowed to erode, doubts can grow about their importance, and further deterioration becomes more likely. Walter Wriston emphasized this point:

For me, what has to be consistent is that you run your business in an honest, straightforward way. For someone who says, "If we pay this guy with a Rolex watch, we'll get the order," the answer is simply, "No, we never do that." If you don't act that way, all the values fray around the edges.

The price can be much higher than simple vigilance. Almost every manager can find himself or herself in situations in which a commitment to important intangibles directly conflicts with short-term performance or profits. Being right and being profitable are not always the same thing. These moments are highly visible. They set precedents that can constrain a manager and influence a company for years. There is no simple formula for resolving individual cases. But it is clear that one of the most powerful ways to make intangibles tangible is to be willing to pay a price—an explicit, significant price—rather than abandon them.

After he became president of a rather sleepy, $30-million company, one manager we know paid such a price. He knew that the company's complacent culture had to change if it was to survive the intensely cost-competitive, recessionary years of the early 1980s. The manager's personal finances were also at stake because part of the compensation package entitled him to purchase shares of stock, which tied up much of his own net worth. He told the board that hired him that he would need time to bring about changes in the company. He acknowledged that he could bring in more competent people from the outside, and do so right away. He even acknowledged that this would build a stronger organization—certainly in the near term, and most likely for the long term. But an overriding personal value of this manager was fair treatment. He recollected:

Early in my career, I had two different jobs. On each of them, I thought I had done pretty good work, but both times I was demoted. No one told me what I did wrong or how I could do better. I don't want to repeat that here. I want to be sure that everyone who wants to be on the team has a fair chance to play.

He told the board that if they hired him, he would take a slower, gentler, more patient approach to changing the company's culture. He believed that many of the managers he would inherit had never had the opportunity to learn to do their jobs in a competent, professional way. He intended to make it clear from the beginning that there would be a major change in the way the company did business. He was willing to be patient, however, and even forgiving with those who might take time becoming comfortable and confident under his new regime. This manager's commitment to his values cost him time, effort, and money. Ultimately, his efforts paid off, and he led the company into a long period of profitable growth.

This example reflects a situation in which intangible concerns internal to the company are in conflict with external concerns that are equally difficult to measure and whose consequences are equally difficult to predict. Internally, the employees argued that they liked their work, their low-stress work environment, their close relationships with their customers, and the ability to be home with their families in the evenings. To them, the company's ways were a key to the good life. Externally, however, the competitive realities were real: the need to counter a Japanese threat and the need to increase profit margins to finance manufacturing improvements and new product development. To meet these threats, employees would need to work longer hours and negotiate harder with customers, jeopardizing the close relationships they had enjoyed.

INTANGIBLES AND INTEGRITY

The lesson here is a broad one. The widespread, Pollyanna-ish view that commitment to lofty goals and values is a sure and safe road to outstanding performance naively implies that tangibles and intangibles never collide and that painful trade-offs need not be made. Unfortunately, the world is not arranged so serendipitously. When managers *do* pay a price for their commitment to integrity—to their long-term strategic visions, high ethical standards, and abiding company values—they have the comfort of knowing that they have clearly set an example and a precedent that will reinforce these intangibles throughout their organizations.

There is a final consideration. While a leader must be the catalyst in making intangibles real, one person cannot shoulder this work alone. The larger the company, the truer this is. Leaders must therefore look for reinforcement. They must take special care in recruiting employees who seem to share the intangible values that they believe are critical. This often means that the company president must take an active role in interviewing and selecting candidates for jobs, even at lower levels in the company.

Building a commitment to intangibles also means promoting people based on criteria that extend beyond their technical competence or even their management and implementation skills. Becoming a "member of the team" or a "member of the family" means that people who rise in a company's hierarchy share the commitment to the intangibles that the team and the leader value. The managers who become part of the senior executive team *must* share these values; the leader of an organization, especially of a large and complicated company, simply does not have the time to communicate, defend, and set a personal example reinforcing these values to all the employees in the company.

Managers play for very high stakes when tangible and intangible factors collide. These issues can involve trade-offs between any combination of long-term strategic vision, short-term economic concerns, deep-rooted company norms and values, and personal values and self-interest. Many of these conflicts are embodied in the conflicts among priorities given to the interests of different constituent groups. Since these issues usually matter a great deal to many members of the organization, they are often highly visible and quite emotional. They are not just technical, economic matters which, because they are susceptible to cost-benefit analysis, are more likely to be viewed dispassionately. In contrast, people care personally about the intangibles and the way they are re-solved. The way managers handle these intangibles can funda-mentally affect their effectiveness and credibility; such deci-sions reflect leaders' personal integrity and courage. For this reason, their decisions can communicate conviction or vacil-lation on issues that matter deeply to many other members of the organization, and their decisions can influence how much trust others are willing to place in them.

The implications of our prejudice for this dilemma are clear: in many ways intangibles lie at the heart of the effort to achieve integrity of action, organizational aims, and per-sonal belief. Unless a leader acts forcefully to counter the tyr-anny of the tangibles, his or her personal values will become diffuse in the eyes of subordinates and organizational aims will lack qualities that are essential to securing strong commit-ments, to stimulating effort, and to guiding action.

NOTE

1. Christopher A. Bartlett, "Komatsu Limited," 385–277. Boston: Harvard Business School, 1985, p. 15.

Chapter 9

<u>INTEGRITY IN ACTION</u>

The conflicts among the three philosophies of leadership raise two questions for managers: Which view or combination of views gives the best guidance to managers who want to become leaders? Or, should managers ignore all three and instead simply do what seems to make the most sense in each situation? In the last five chapters, we have offered answers to both questions.

We conclude that to be most effective, managers should avoid the seductions of the "style" school. Instead, they should strive to be consistent across situations and their behavior should be consonant with their personalities, beliefs, and judgments. Furthermore, managers should approach the situations they face with a specific set of predispositions or prejudices.

In making this argument, we have parted company with the widespread view that the right behavior for a manager in any situation depends entirely on the particulars of the situation, that is, on the company's strategy, its organization structure and systems, and the politics and personalities involved. This popular view misleadingly transforms the contingency theory of organization—the view that the right way to organize, plan, control, and motivate depends on a company's strategy—into a chameleon view of leadership. What is sound advice for the designing of managerial systems and structures is bad advice for managers' behavior.

Nor, by itself, does any one of the three philosophies suffice. Hence the prejudices meld together the directive and values-driven philosophies of leadership. Sometimes a changing market dictates that a company's values must change. This requires that a leader take powerful, direct, personal action. Because values sometimes float serenely above pressing daily realities, leaders need to take strong, consistent action to make them real, vivid, and effective. At other times, when the force of daily realities pressures people to compromise values, a company needs clear, forceful, and consistent leadership to defend and further promote the threatened values. Directive leadership meets these needs. Yet it misses the insight of the values-driven philosophy: companies are communities, not just economic instruments; when they meet the higher needs and aspirations of their members, they can elicit extraordinary commitment, effort, and creativity.

The prejudices do not ignore the political philosophy. Its tough-minded realism is the reason managers should follow prejudices and not rules. At times, outstanding leaders do resolve dilemmas in ways consistent with the philosophy of political leadership, and they are right to do so. But the political approach is hazardous for the long term. The surer path to leadership lies in the directive and values-driven approaches. This means being clear and precise and confronting conflicts directly. It means encouraging bottom-up influence while retaining the ability to get directly involved. It involves being preoccupied with substance, not process, and making persistent efforts to help intangibles overcome the tyranny of the tangible.

With these guidelines, many managers should have leadership within their grasp. They have character, intelligence, and experience. They want to make a significant difference in their companies. They know that this will be satisfying to do, rewarding to look back on, and open even greater opportunities in the future. The path to leadership is hardly obscure. The prejudices we have described are straightforward.

Why Is Leadership Rare?

Yet leadership remains uncommon. Why? Organizations must accept some blame. Unfortunately, the way many companies are managed slowly but surely conditions people to give up their leadership traits. Rigidity, routines, and norms dampen initiative. As most people can attest from personal experience, many individuals enter companies with drive, energy, and ideas—attributes commonly associated with leadership—only to have unchallenged conventional wisdom, the emphasis on specialization and technique, bureaucratic processes, political infighting, and the erosive pressure of day-to-day problems stifle their leadership abilities. In this sense, leadership can be *unlearned*. Also some organizations are simply sick. Cautious, political behavior has metastasized like cancer throughout them. In these cases, the right approach is usually to get out.

But often the fault lies in ourselves. Some of us adhere to misguided assumptions about human behavior. We have inadequate faith in the abilities of others or we view human motivation only in terms of the self-interested pursuit of power, money, and security. We fail to recognize that people are also motivated by a need to create and a desire to serve worthwhile ends.

Very often the main problem is simply a lack of courage. Not the valor of grand, heroic acts, but determination and honesty practiced daily in the small situations and familiar dilemmas of managerial life; the courage to do and say what one believes to be right, rather than what is convenient, familiar, or popular; the courage to act on one's vision for his or her organization. In this respect, the approaches of political and directive leadership are dramatically different. According to Abraham Zaleznik, the predisposition to negotiate and compromise has different psychological roots from the directive leader's predisposition to act boldly:

> [Political] managers tend to be afraid of aggression as a force leading to chaos. Yet aggression is innate in human beings and must be allowed to assume its part in work. Indeed, there can be no useful work without the release of aggression. The key element in what leaders do for followers is to show them how to release aggression in constructive ways and toward desirable ends.[1]

Courage helps managers resist the many pressures to accede to the demands of particular situations. These pressures are powerful and familiar: thus the Japanese saying "The nail that sticks up gets hammered down." Although Americans take pride in their individuality, they often fear being wrong, standing out, taking responsibility, disappointing others, or making the boss unhappy and so go along with the group and leave the battle for another day. This temptation is especially strong when managers face complicated, ambiguous problems for which there is no clear right answer. Then almost any viewpoint is subject to criticism, and rather than think an issue through for one's self and take a stand, it is more comfortable to be cautious or even equivocal.

Leadership requires the courage to resist the pressures of immediate situations. There are two reasons for this, each intertwined with the other. One lies in the hazards of letting situations dominate, the other in the power of consistency.

The Pitfalls of Situational Management

The situational approach holds that almost everything is flexible and can be adapted to the demands of situations, including a manager's "style." Those who work with such managers sense that they often try to manage perceptions and create impressions, even when these differ from what they really think or believe. Their behavior is premeditated and calculated, rather than spontaneous and natural. At its extreme, this approach results in a polished acting job in which the performer behaves in ways that may not be consistent with his or her personality, values, and thinking.

Moreover, when these managers explain their actions, or advise others, they stress the perceptions, interests, and power of the parties in a situation. They take a pragmatic, skeptical, somewhat cynical view of people, organizations, and the path to getting ahead in a company. At the extreme, they live out of emotional suitcases from which they take different behavior, like changes of clothing. Those who work for them often wonder "just whom are they trying to kid?"

Of course, allowing situations to dominate behavior can be effective, in a low-grade way. It can help capable people achieve adequacy, especially in the middle levels of large, bureaucratic organizations. But it is a winding, perilous path to leadership.

Simply acceding to the demands of situations sets a poor example. Members of a company, a department, or a small team look to their managers to learn what kind of behavior will help them get ahead. If they think that decisions and behavior shaped by immediate pressures lead to success, most will act this way. When this way of acting holds sway, organizations—which already have natural, inertial tendencies to become cautious and political—become complicated political arenas. No one knows how decisions will be made in the future. That depends on the pressures, now unknown, that will be at work. Trust and confidence erode, second-guessing of decisions increases, and elaborate systems have to be put in place to rein in self-interested behavior. In short, senior managers' political behavior reproduces itself, and its progeny can be a political, cumbersome organization. The leaders we interviewed were plainly hostile to political tendencies. Alexander d'Arbeloff said:

> The chief executive sets the tone, and the tone I've set is antipolitical. Politics have no place here, and I just won't tolerate it. You treat people with dignity; you don't manipulate them. The whole organization knows I feel that way.

The situational approach creates other risks. Even the best managers make mistakes, and the consequences are much more serious for practitioners of flexible style. It is far better to fail after a straightforward, honest attempt based on substantive analysis of the business issues, than to fail after trying to subtly manage perceptions and appearances. In the latter case, people view a manager as a failed politician. His or her credibility erodes, and people will interpret future actions as insincere, untrustworthy, and unfair. By contrast, a manager who fails but followed, with sincerity, the prejudices for substance, clarity, and fairness will not be tarnished by mistrust. In the final analysis, good work and honest effort are the best politics.

Once a manager's decisions are viewed as the vector sum of immediate pressures, people intensify the pressures that serve their interests. As a result, a situation-minded manager's work gets much more difficult. Astonishingly, managers who pride themselves on their subtle maneuvering and hardheaded, often cynical realism make the naive assumption that the people around them do not spend a great deal of time deciphering the managers' latest twist or turn and trying to influence the next one.

The situational approach offers a false simplicity: just determine the behavior required by the situation and adapt accordingly. In reality, such advice increases the complexity of the manager's job. The number of possible situations with varying stakes and competitive pressures is infinite. Managers, like weather vanes, must then adapt to ever-shifting sets of political interests and economic requirements. Not only must they sort out all the complexities and uncertainties of today's competitive environment, but also they must spend an inordinate amount of time and energy trying to see through the maneuvering that surrounds them. Because some of the information they get—how much they do not know—has been massaged for political advantage, its quality deteriorates. As conflicts become grounded in local self-interest rather than differences of opinion over substantive business issues, they intensify and become more personal. Finally, if a manager is surrounded by people who are reluctant to put their cards on the table and be candid, simply because they believe that that is not the way in which decisions are made in the company, shared purpose becomes far more difficult to achieve.

Paradoxically, preoccupation with the immediate situation, which supposedly increases the manager's flexibility, proves in practice to create inflexibility. A manager's ability to affect outcomes in a wide range of situations is the measure of true flexibility. Vagueness and imprecision make it hard for others to understand a manager's commitment to a course of action. Consequently, the manager then has less influence on what others do, making it difficult to get a company to react quickly and precisely to new challenges. By contrast, when managers are specific and consistent about goals, expectations, and evaluations, and when they foster an environment of trust, commitment, and respect, people can respond to external events and implement decisions more quickly and accurately.

An easy counter to this criticism of political-minded, situational leadership is that it applies only to managers who are not very good at varying their style. Even the advocates of this approach readily admit that few managers are capable of doing it very well. Indeed, that is one of the themes of the political philosophy of leadership: it requires unusual skills, which must be practiced and learned over years. But the weakness in this line of thinking is its gross underestimate of the real difficulty of sustaining political leadership over a long period of time and of the inherent conflicts between the assumptions upon which it is founded and the behavior followers respond to most favorably.

If a manager has peers, bosses, and subordinates who are intelligent, perceptive people, and if he or she works with them day by day on challenging problems, they will all come to know who the manager really is. A person would need extraordinarily sophisticated acting skills to fool or manipulate through chameleon-like behavior a large number of intelligent people over a long period of time. (According to Abraham Lincoln, it cannot be done.) Managers who readily adapt their styles in ways that are inconsistent with their personalities risk being perceived as inconsistent, and possibly insincere, hypocritical, and manipulative. Inconsistency is likely to lead to erroneous perceptions and expectations by followers. It simply is less clear what the leader stands for and wants. Inconsistent actions blur the communication of the company's purpose and goals, breed suspicion of the leader's sincerity and commitment to the company's purpose, and potentially erode critical values such as trust, loyalty, and fairness. Deception and insincerity are not raw materials for leadership.

Integrity Born of Consistency

Consistency is not using a cookie cutter or rigid rules for decisions and actions. The prejudices acknowledge that many things a manager does must vary depending on the situation. Depending on the task at hand, its strategic importance, the urgency of the matter, and the ability of the people to whom the task is delegated, executives will delegate more or less. Executives also have to vary their approach to motivating different groups of people.

Consistency means that the same personal values and organizational aims will powerfully influence what a manager does and says. Integrity in managerial action means these guideposts should not vary. The prejudices we have described directly reflect the personal aspirations and organizational aims that link integrity and leadership. The predispositions with which managers approach a situation greatly affect their evaluation of the issues, the alternatives that they identify, and the decisions that they make. For example, a preoccupation with the stakes and perceptions of the people involved in a situation can easily crowd out concern for the economic substance of an issue and the values potentially at stake.

This is why commitment to high ethical standards and to a vision for a company must remain firm, regardless of situational pressures. Respect for others, demanding standards, and expectations of candor must all remain constant. Preoccupation with substance should not give way to the shifting tides of varying situations.

We have argued for consistency among personal values, organizational aims, and personal actions. The critical element of leadership is behavior that bonds certain values and aims. It is action that imprints them on an organization. Hence, this book has concentrated on integrity of action as expressed by the three philosophies and then the prejudices.

Consistency of action is important for a variety of reasons. First, for values to matter, a leader must consistently defend and promote them. The widespread cynicism toward institutions today means that many key corporate values are very fragile. The slightest compromise can undermine them. Compromise can justify followers' innate skepticism and causes subordinates to view management's commitment to key values as shallow at best, probably hypocritical, and possibly manipulative. Commitment to values requires consistency. Values cannot be institutionalized through compromise.

Second, a consistent set of prejudices can produce real synergies. The prejudices we described reinforce each other, clarifying and strengthening a leader's efforts. Some prejudices can compensate for the risks of others. For example, a single-minded prejudice for bottom-up influence and autonomy can provide the opportunity for localitis to flourish. Clarity in goals and expectations, however, checks this tendency, as do a capability for top-down intervention and a company culture that values trust and openness.

Third, inconsistent behavior sends mixed signals to subordinates, increasing anxiety-producing uncertainty, raising concerns about fairness, confusing the nature and priority of goals, and raising the possibility that a leader will be seen as being deceptively manipulative. A leader must be constantly aware of the danger that others may interpret actions differently than he or she intends. It is followers' interpretations that are most important to leadership. Consistent behavior is the best antidote to damaging misreadings.

Finally, not only do the inconsistencies created by excessive flexibility and adaptability limit how flexible a person *should* be, but a person's personality, beliefs, assumptions, and skills limit how flexible he or she *can* be. Most people are predisposed by personality and beliefs to a certain view of leadership and to a set of prejudices that are part of that view. Some people's personality and ability naturally give them a wider range of effective behavior than others have, but no one is unconstrained by personal limitations. Style is not something of choice to be altered at will without consequence. The most effective business leaders are not human chameleons, but rather are people of distinctive personalities who behave consistently in accordance with that personality. To do otherwise invites mistrust and mistakes. Actions alien to one's personality take the manager into an area where instinct and "gut feel" are no longer as operative. Judgment, therefore, is diminished.

To appreciate the power of consistency ask yourself what kind of values and behavior you want in the people who work for you. Do you want them to bring you bad news on a timely basis and in plain, unvarnished form? Or would you prefer subordinates who are adept at "managing upward," and who will convey bad news or recommend opportunities only after waiting for and then orchestrating the right situation in which to convey it? Do you want the people who work for you to be preoccupied with substance or with process? With confronting problems squarely or with deflecting them or compromising them away? Do you want their ethical standards to be high or low? And do you want those who work for you to follow these prejudices consistently or occasionally?

The answers to these questions are clear. Managers need to hear the facts, clearly and plainly, from others. These candid assessments may not always be pleasant, but it is better to have them than not. Candor need not be blunt or harsh. Civility and tact are virtues. But neither can candor always be painless. It is a scarce, sometimes precious, commodity. It is wise to think twice before using the inevitable conflicts and pressures of situations as excuses for delaying, deflecting, or massaging the facts of the situation or for lowering ethical commitments.

The prejudices we have advocated are an alternative to vacillating like a weather vane in reaction to the immediate pressures of every situation. They aim at consistency, but not the foolish consistency of treating all people and problems according to the same formula, nor the mistake of treating everything like a nail because one happens to have a hammer. What matters for managers is consistency born of abiding commitment to certain personal values and certain organizational aims and to guiding actions by their lights.

Leadership in a world of dilemmas is not, fundamentally, a matter of style, charisma, or professional management technique. It is a difficult daily quest for integrity. Managers' behavior should be an unadorned, consistent reflection of what they believe and what they aspire to for a company. Managers who take this approach earn trust. Commitment to leadership through integrity can help managers through the inevitable periods of anxiety, doubt, and trial, and give them a sense of priorities to guide them through an uncertain world.

In the final analysis, the power of executive leadership rests not so much on the personality of the individual as on the power of the ideas, purposes, and values he or she represents. Leaders are agents and catalysts through which others understand and identify with these ideas, purposes, and values, and are uplifted and motivated by them. When this occurs, a leader's efforts are amplified and focused in ways that enhance a company's competitive advantages and help it to serve society.

NOTE

1. From a draft of Chapter 1 of a forthcoming book by Abraham Zaleznik, *The Managerial Mystique: Changing Realities of Business Leadership.*

BIBLIOGRAPHY

Abegglen, James C. *Kaisha, The Japanese Corporation.* New York: Basic Books, 1985.

Ackoff, Russell L. *Management in Small Doses.* New York: John Wiley, 1986.

Aisner, James E. "A Premium on Scholarship." *Harvard Business School Bulletin,* February 1985, pp. 58–67.

Allison, Graham T. *Essence of Decision: Explaining the Cuban Missile Crisis.* Boston: Little, Brown, 1971.

Andrews, Kenneth R. *The Concept of Corporate Strategy.* Rev. ed. Homewood, IL: Richard D. Irwin, 1980.

Auletta, Ken. *The Art of Corporate Success.* New York: Penguin, 1983.

Barnard, Chester. *The Functions of the Executive.* Cambridge, MA: Harvard University Press, 1938.

Bass, Bernard M. *Stogdil's Handbook of Leadership.* New York: Free Press, 1981.

———. *Leadership and Performance Beyond Expectations.* New York: Free Press, 1985.

Bennis, Warren G. *Changing Organizations: Essays on the Development and Evolution of Human Organization.* New York: McGraw-Hill, 1966.

Bennis, Warren G., and Burt Nanus. *Leaders: The Strategies for Taking Charge.* New York: Harper & Row, 1985.

Berg, Norman. "The Allocation of Strategic Funds in a Large Diversified Company." Ph.D. diss., Harvard Business School, 1963.

———. *General Management: An Analytical Approach.* Homewood, IL: Richard D. Irwin, 1984.

Berger, Peter L. "Some General Observations on the Problem of Work." In *The Human Shape of Work,* ed. Peter L. Berger. New York: Macmillan, 1964, pp. 211–239.

Bower, Joseph L. *Managing the Resource Allocation Process.* Boston: Division of Research, Harvard Business School, 1970.

———. *The Two Faces of Management.* Boston: Houghton Mifflin, 1983.

Bower, Marvin. *The Will to Manage.* New York: McGraw-Hill, 1966.

Braybrooke, David, and Charles E. Lindblom. *A Strategy of Decision: Policy Evaluation as a Social Process.* New York: Free Press, 1963.

Burns, James MacGregor. *Leadership.* New York: Harper & Row, 1978.

Chandler, Alfred D., Jr. *Strategy and Structure: Chapters in the History of the American Industrial Enterprise.* Cambridge: MA: MIT Press, 1962.

————. The Visible Hand: The Managerial Revolution in American Business. Cambridge, MA: Harvard University Press, 1977.

Christensen, C. Roland. "Education for the General Manager." Unpublished working paper, Harvard Business School, no date.

Christensen, C. Roland, Kenneth R. Andrews, and Joseph L. Bower. Business Policy: Text and Cases, 4th ed. Homewood, IL: Richard D. Irwin, 1978.

Christensen, C. Roland, et al. Policy Formulation and Administration. Homewood, IL: Richard D. Irwin, 1985.

Cohen, Michael D., and James G. March. Leadership and Ambiguity, 2d ed. Boston: Harvard Business School Press, 1986.

Collier, Abram T. "Business Leadership and a Creative Society." Harvard Business Review, January–February 1968, pp. 154–156.

Crozier, Michael. The Bureaucratic Phenomenon. Chicago: University of Chicago Press, 1964.

Cyert, Richard M., and James G. March. A Behavioral Theory of the Firm. Englewood Cliffs, NJ: Prentice-Hall, 1963.

Donaldson, Gordon, and Jay W. Lorsch. Decision Making at the Top. New York: Basic Books, 1983.

Drucker, Peter F. Concept of the Corporation. New York: John Day, 1946.

————. The Practice of Management. New York: Harper & Row, 1954.

————. Management: Task, Responsibilities, Practices. New York: Harper & Row, 1973.

————. Innovation and Entrepreneurship. New York: Harper & Row, 1985.

————. "The Coming of the New Organization." Harvard Business Review, January–February 1988, pp. 45–53.

Ellsworth, Richard R. "Capital Markets and Comparative Decline." Harvard Business Review, September–October 1985, pp. 171–183.

————. "Subordinate Financial Policy to Corporate Strategy." Harvard Business Review, November–December 1983, pp. 170–182.

Fromm, Eric. The Sane Society. New York: Fawcett World Library, 1955.

Galbraith, John Kenneth. The New Industrial State. Boston: Houghton Mifflin, 1967.

Gardner, John W. Self-Renewal. New York: Harper & Row, 1971.

————. Leadership Paper Series. Washington, D.C.: Independent Sector, 1986.

Geneen, Harold. Managing. Garden City, NY: Doubleday, 1984.

Gouldner, Alvin W. Studies in Leadership. New York: Russell & Russell, 1965.

Greenleaf, Robert K. Servant Leadership: A Journey into the Nature of Legitimate Power and Greatness. New York: Paulist Press, 1977.

Halberstam, David. The Best and the Brightest. New York: Random House, 1972.

Herzberg, Frederick. Work and the Nature of Man. Cleveland: World, 1966.

Hirschman, Albert O. Exit, Voice and Loyalty. Cambridge, MA: Harvard University Press, 1970.

Homans, George C. *The Human Group.* New York: Harcourt, Brace, 1950.
―――. *Social Behavior: Its Elementary Forms.* New York: Harcourt Brace Jovanovich, 1961.
Isenberg, Daniel J. "How Senior Managers Think." *Harvard Business Review,* November–December 1984, pp. 81–90.
Janis, Irving L., and Leon Mann. *Decision Making.* New York: Free Press, 1977.
Kanter, Rosabeth Moss. *Men and Women of the Corporation.* New York: Basic Books, 1977.
―――. *The Change Masters.* New York: Simon and Schuster, 1983.
Katz, Daniel, and Robert L. Kahn. *The Social Psychology of Organizations.* New York: John Wiley, 1966.
Kotter, John P. *The General Managers.* New York: Free Press, 1982.
―――. *Power and Influence.* New York: Free Press, 1985.
―――. *The Leadership Factor.* New York: Free Press, 1988.
Lawrence, Paul R., and Jay W. Lorsch. *Organization and Environment.* Boston: Division of Research, Harvard Business School, 1967.
Lax, David A., and James K. Sebenius. *The Manager as Negotiator.* New York: Free Press, 1986.
Leavitt, Harold J. *Corporate Pathfinders.* Homewood, IL: Dow Jones-Irwin, 1986.
Levinson, Harry. *CEO: Corporate Leadership in Action.* New York: Basic Books, 1984.
Likert, Rensis. *The Human Organization.* New York: McGraw-Hill, 1967.
Lilienthal, David E. *Management: A Humanist Art.* New York: Columbia University Press, 1967.
Lindbloom, Charles E. "The Science of Muddling Through." *Public Administration Review* 19 (1959), pp. 79–88.
―――. *The Policy-Making Process.* Englewood Cliffs, NJ: Prentice-Hall, 1968.
Livingston, J. S. "Myth of the Well-Educated Manager." *Harvard Business Review,* January–February 1971, pp. 79–89.
―――. *Executive.* Cambridge, MA: Harvard University Press, 1981.
Lodge, George C. *The New American Ideology.* New York: Alfred A. Knopf, 1975.
―――. *The American Disease.* New York: Alfred A. Knopf, 1984.
Maccoby, Michael. *The Gamesman.* New York: Simon and Schuster, 1976.
Machiavelli, Nicolo. *The Prince.* Translated by Luigi Ricci, revised by E.R.P. Vincent. New York: Mentor Press, 1962.
McClelland, David. *The Achieving Society.* New York: Van Nostrand, 1961.
McGregor, Douglas. *The Human Side of Enterprise.* New York: McGraw-Hill, 1960.
March, James, and Herbert Simon. *Organizations.* New York: John Wiley, 1958.
Marx, Karl. *Selected Writings.* Edited by David McLellan. Oxford: Oxford University Press, 1977.

Maslow, Abraham H. "A Theory of Human Motivation." *Psychological Review* 50 (1943), pp. 370–396.

———. *Motivation and Personality.* New York: Harper & Row, 1954.

Miles, Robert E., and Charles C. Snow. *Organizational Strategy, Structure, and Process.* New York: McGraw-Hill, 1978.

Mintzberg, Henry. *The Nature of Managerial Work.* New York: Harper & Row, 1973.

———. "Strategy-Making in Three Modes." *California Management Review,* Winter 1973, pp. 44–53.

———. "The Manager's Job: Folklore and Fact." *Harvard Business Review,* July–August 1975, pp. 49–61.

———. *The Structuring of Organizations.* Englewood Cliffs, NJ: Prentice-Hall, 1979.

———. *Power In and Around Organizations.* Englewood Cliffs, NJ: Prentice-Hall, 1983.

Neustadt, Richard E. *Presidential Power: The Politics of Leadership.* New York: John Wiley, 1960.

Niebuhr, Reinhold. *Moral Man and Immoral Society.* New York: Scribner's & Sons, 1932.

Nozick, Robert. *Anarchy, State, and Utopia.* New York: Basic Books, 1974.

Ouchi, William G. *Theory Z: How American Business Can Meet the Japanese Challenge.* Reading, MA: Addison-Wesley, 1981.

Pascale, Richard T., and Anthony G. Athos. *The Art of Japanese Management.* New York: Simon and Schuster, 1981.

Patton, George S., Jr. *War As I Know It.* Boston: Houghton Mifflin, 1947.

Peters, Thomas J., and Robert H. Waterman, Jr. *In Search of Excellence.* New York: Harper & Row, 1982.

Pfeffer, Jeffrey. *Power in Organizations.* Marshfield, MA: Pitman Publishing, 1981.

Quinn, James Brian. "Managing Innovation: Controlled Chaos." *Harvard Business Review,* May–June 1985, pp. 73–84.

Raiffa, Howard. *The Art & Science of Negotiation.* Cambridge, MA: Harvard University Press, 1982.

Rawls, John. *A Theory of Justice.* Cambridge, MA: Harvard University Press, Belknap Press, 1971.

Riesman, David. *The Lonely Crowd.* New Haven: Yale University Press, 1950.

Roethlisberger, Fritz, and W. Dickson. *Management and the Worker.* Cambridge, MA: Harvard University Press, 1939.

Sathe, Vijay. *Culture and Related Corporate Realities.* Homewood, IL: Richard D. Irwin, 1985.

Sayles, Leonard. *Managerial Behavior: Administration in Complex Organizations.* New York: McGraw-Hill, 1964.

———. *Leadership: What Effective Managers Really Do. . .and How They Do It.* New York: McGraw-Hill, 1979.

Schein, Edgar H. *Organizational Culture and Leadership*. San Francisco: Jossey-Bass, 1985.

Schelling, Thomas C. *The Strategy of Conflict*. London: Oxford University Press, 1963.

Schlesinger, Arthur M., Jr. *The Coming of the New Deal*. Boston: Houghton Mifflin, 1958.

Schumpeter, Joseph. *The Theory of Economic Development*. Cambridge, MA: Harvard University Press, 1934.

———. *Capitalism, Socialism, and Democracy*. New York: Harper Bros., 1942.

Sculley, John. *Odyssey*. New York: Harper & Row, 1987.

Selznick, Philip. *Leadership in Administration*. New York: Harper & Row, 1957.

Simon, Herbert A. *Administrative Behavior*, 3d ed. New York: Free Press, 1976.

Sloan, Alfred P., Jr. *My Years With General Motors*. Garden City, NY: Anchor Books, 1972.

Steiner, George A. *Strategic Planning: What Every Manager Must Know*. New York: Free Press, 1979.

Stewart, Rosemary. *Managers and Their Jobs*. London: Macmillan, 1967.

Tannenbaum, Robert, and Warren H. Schmidt. "How to Choose a Leadership Pattern." *Harvard Business Review*, May–June 1973, pp. 162–183.

Vancil, Richard F. "Strategy Formulation in Complex Organizations." *Sloan Management Review*, Winter 1976, pp. 1–18.

———. *Decentralization: Managerial Ambiguity by Design*. Homewood, IL: Dow Jones-Irwin, 1979.

———. *Implementing Strategy: The Role of Top Management*. Boston: Division of Research, Harvard Business School, 1981.

Watson, Thomas J., Jr. *A Business and Its Beliefs*. New York: McGraw-Hill, 1963.

Weber, Max. *The Protestant Ethic and the Spirit of Capitalism*. Translated by Talcott Parsons. New York: Charles Scribner's Sons, 1930.

———. *The Theory of Social and Economic Organization*. New York: Oxford University Press, 1947.

Whyte, William F. *Street Corner Society*. Chicago: University of Chicago Press, 1955.

Williamson, Oliver E. *Markets and Hierarchies*. New York: Harper & Row, 1966.

Wrapp, H. Edward. "Good Managers Don't Make Policy Decisions." *Harvard Business Review*, September–October 1967, pp. 91–99.

Yankelovich, Daniel. "The Work Ethic Is Underemployed." *Psychology Today*, May 1982, pp. 5–6.

Yoshino, Michael. *Japan's Managerial System: Tradition and Innovation*. Cambridge, MA: MIT Press, 1968.

Yukl, Gary A. *Leadership in Organizations.* Englewood Cliffs, NJ: Prentice-Hall, 1981.

Zaleznik, Abraham. *Human Dilemmas of Leadership.* New York: Harper & Row, 1966.

———. "Power and Politics in Organizational Life." *Harvard Business Review,* May–June 1970, pp. 47–60.

———. "Managers and Leaders: Are They Different?" *Harvard Business Review,* May–June 1977, pp. 67–88.

———. "The Leadership Gap." *Washington Quarterly* 6 (1983): pp. 32–39.

———. *The Managerial Mystique: Changing Realities of Business Leadership.* Forthcoming.

Zaleznik, Abraham, and Manfred Kets De Vries. *Power and the Corporate Mind.* Boston: Houghton Mifflin, 1975.

Index

ABOUT THE AUTHORS

Joseph L. Badaracco is Professor of Business Administration at Harvard Business School.

Richard R. Ellsworth is Associate Professor of Management at The Claremont Graduate School.